GW01453086

The
Politically-Correct
Gospel

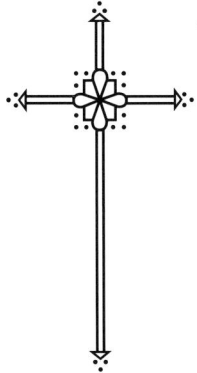

The
Politically-Correct
Gospel

Peter Mullen

THE
SOCIAL
AFFAIRS
UNIT

ISBN 1-904863-17-5

Social Affairs Unit
314-322 Regent Street
London W1B 5SA
www.socialaffairsunit.org.uk

ACKNOWLEDGEMENTS

I would like to thank Michael Mosbacher
of the Social Affairs Unit for indulging my sense of humour.
He that hath ears to hear, let him hear.

THE AUTHOR

The Rev Dr Peter Mullen is Rector of St Michael, Cornhill
and Chaplain to the Stock Exchange.

His most recent books include
Holy Smoke: Tales of a City Rector
Everyday Thoughts and
Minute Sermons.

These publications are all available from:

The St Michael's Foundation
The Watch House
10 Giltspur Street
London EC1A 9DE

PREFACE BY THE
ARCHBISHOPS AND BISHOPS

Of course, many will ask what need there is of a new gospel. It seems surely sacrilegious to think to add to – let alone improve upon – the sublime narratives given us by Matthew, Mark, Luke and John. And the attempt would be, at the very least, a waste of time and effort. This is, indeed, a strong criticism and must be answered directly, without qualms about all those outmoded notions of respect and reverence.

So, then, it must be said at the outset that, on all the really important issues concerning human life and happiness, the gospel writers, St Paul and Jesus himself were hopelessly misguided. We should not blame them for their ignorance – for, after all, they did not have the benefit of the Enlightenment, or of the positive and progressive philosophies of Karl Marx, of the whole Christian Socialist Movement, and lacked the psychological insights of Freud. The more recent developments in progressive understanding, and the whole liberation being worked by modernisation and Political-Correctness, far exceed the primitive and limited understanding of Jesus of Nazareth, who was a man of his time (and no more than an Israeli anyhow).

We are aware that there are those who will object that our present-day modernisers – ourselves included – are also but men of their time. And to these critics we say, sadly and solemnly, that we are not much given to such unfavourable comparisons.

But it does little good to generalise, and so we must substantiate the case for modernity over and against the so-called traditional and historic gospel. To begin with, it should not be assumed that there is any such tradition – for the Church itself has not, for the last two centuries, believed the original gospels.

To its credit, the modern Church has seen those primitive events which were formerly misunderstood as "miracles" as entirely superstitious and as, at best, involving a metaphorical and "demythologised" interpretation. To take just two examples: first, the primitive proclamation of the so-called "Resurrection of Christ" can now clearly be understood as a form of synecdochic and metonymic expression of the "truth" that the disciples experienced a new and liberated socialist consciousness after Jesus had been put to death. And second, the Blessed Sacrament of the Holy Communion is self-evidently a metaphor for Fair Trade coffee.

But, as we are always being accused of taking refuge in abstractions, let us turn to specifics.

First, there is the irritating and unreconstructed, unenlightened way in which Jesus Christ used to speak of sin. We are embarrassed that we should even have to employ such an outdated word – for what could it possibly mean, except that someone failed to support modern and corporate attempts, such as by the United Nations, to liberate us from the primitive evils of national chauvinism?

And on the individual, personal, level we understand, since Marx and Freud, that what used to be called "sin" – together with much that was mistakenly referred to as "personal responsibility" – is, in fact, the product of the social coercion of a patriarchal and capitalist society and, of course, of unconscious forces. So, again to give an example: it was recently reported in the capitalist press that a young man had murdered his rich parents in the knowledge that he would inherit their wealth. In the bad old days, such a "crime" would have been reprehended as the act, as we have even heard it described, of "a selfish little prat". Now, though, we know that the so-called "perpetrator" was suffering from Narcissistic Personality Disorder and so (in the circumstances) was quite powerless to do anything except slaughter his parents.

In short, Jesus condemned "self-esteem": we realise his mistake and promote it.

Regrettably, in the teaching of Jesus we find so much of the old-fashioned notion that there is such a thing as personal responsibility, and even that the so-called "unrepentant sinner" might be con-

8

demned to hell. Since Freud, though, we understand that talk of "decency" and "goodness" is merely bourgeois morality and really filthy rags. Moreover, the punitive notions of responsibility, condemnation and punishment must be superseded by the psycho-analytic doctrine of positive transference and the political policy of social inclusion.

While we understand, in the full knowledge of modern psychology, that morality and responsibility are but outdated fictions in the areas of sexual behaviour, and that even the idea of the moral agent is bourgeois and primitive, we do insist that Christian people accept and approve the enlightened doctrines of modern social ethics as they apply to the collective.

In short, while we do not for one moment accept that, in the case of what was formerly referred to as "morality", people are personally responsible for individual misdeeds – indeed they cannot be held so responsible for the psychological and economic reasons which Freud and Marx have demonstrated – yet we firmly believe that individuals are responsible for their political and corporate opinions as they affect the collective. So, for example, while a person cannot be responsible for his or her personal sexual morals, he or she is most certainly responsible for his or her racism, sexism or other discriminatory behaviour.

And, should anyone object that a morality which is refused and denied in its individual application shall yet have validity and be binding in its abstract and ideological collective mode, then again we say – after prayerful discussion and much synodical deliberation – we have no interest in the processes of rationality.

When we come to consider those things that make for a happy society and for the place of the totally accepted individual within society, we have to say that Jesus, particularly as represented in those original outmoded gospels, is far too judgmental. To take just one example among a great host, it is said, disgracefully, "He that believeth shall be saved, and he that believeth not shall be damned."

9

We pass over without further comment the tendentious and discriminatory use of the word "he". If Jesus, with all His faults and lack of contemporary insights and enlightenment, felt compelled to make that cruelly exclusivist remark, He might at least have rejected the sexist "he" and said "they".

But to move to the more important point: we now know that, in matters of religious apprehension, there is no question of truth or falsity – let alone the ludicrously primitive and judgmental terms "saved" and "damned". Everything is a matter of opinion. And everyone's opinion is as good as anyone else's. Frankly, we believe that, if Jesus had been all He claimed to be, He would have recognised that fact.

We are saddened by the naivety and, one must say, the irresponsibility of the original four gospels, and for their backwardness and general embodiment of the forces of conservatism, tradition and all false consciousness. The instances are too numerous to mention; suffice it to say that the whole New Testament is verily undermined by them. There is far too much mention of concepts such as "kingdom", "Lord" and, of course, "commandments", all of which reference a primitive and outmoded period before our contemporary enlightenment.

Jesus made appallingly insensitive remarks about "cripples", "the blind", "the deaf and dumb" and "lunatics" – often even in the presence of such people. How crass of him to use the handicap of partial-sightedness – "Can the blind lead the blind?" – to illustrate moral shortcomings. It is evident that he had nothing approaching the medical understanding of today; and any modern psychologist could teach him much about the treatment of those with personality disorders: "possessed by evil spirits" indeed!

And then there is the stricture on divorce and the underlying assumption that marriage is something "designed" to be between one man and one woman for life. This is sexual morality as sexist oppression. In a truly liberated society many sorts of sexual relationships are not only possible but desirable – both heterosexual and homosexual. But Jesus was excessively narrow-minded concerning these matters.

A word on style. While the Archbishops and Bishops are confident that they have produced a gospel that is both acceptable and accessible for our times, they are yet sensitive to the sentimental attachment which many in the Church have to so-called "fine language". In a spirit of conciliation, therefore, while we reject the original gospels as, frankly, unenlightened and discriminatory nonsense, we have, wherever possible, preserved the language of the *King James Bible* and the *Book of Common Prayer* in the hope that this totally modernised and corrected gospel does not occasion too much of a dissociation of sensibility.

In this spirit of correction and true reformation, therefore, we are delighted to commend to the Church and the World this new and much improved gospel for our modern times.

PROLOGUE

In the beginning was the Logo and the Logo was with the Latest Thing, and the Logo was the Latest Thing. The same was in the beginning with the Latest Thing.

All things were made by the Logo; and without the Logo was not anything made that was made.

In him was Glitz; and the Glitz was the oomph of the consumer society. And the Glitz glittereth in the boringness and the boringness comprehendeth it not.

There was this guy sent from the Latest Thing whose name was Jon. The same came for a witness, to bear witness of the Glitz, that all persons indiscriminate as to race, creed or gender might have Lifestyle.

He was not that Glitz, but was sent to do a promo for that Glitz.

That was the glitziest Glitz that turneth on every guy that

cometh into the consumer society. Glitz was in the consumer society, and the consumer society was made by Glitz, but the consumer society getteth not the message.

Glitz came unto his consumers, but his consumers were turned not on by him. But as many as got the message, to them gave he power to become followers of the Latest Thing, even to them that liked the ads on the telly.

Which were born not of fogeyness, nor of the will of the Old Farts, nor of the will of last year's model, but of the Latest Thing.

And the Glitz hit the high street and we beheld its coolness, the coolness as of the only begotten of the Latest Thing full of grooviness and bling.

CHAPTER I

This is the generation of him that is called Moderniser General: And, behold, I looked and saw that there is no generation set down, for the Bureaucrat hath decreed that verily the boasting of genealogy is but a vain thing, sexist and elitist and belongeth rather to the old time which hath passed away.

Now the birth of the Moderniser General was on this wise: when as his mother Rubella was, like, in a meaningful relationship with Wayne (but he knocketh her not off), she was found to be up the duff by the Latest Thing, whose name also is Fashion, Trendy and even Spirit of the Age.

Then Wayne her partner, being a regular sort of guy and not willing to do a runner, trusting that the Child Support Agency would never find him, was minded to tell her not to put herself about on the estate, like, or hang around the disco or the pub and that.

But while he thought on these things, behold, one of the Vibes was sent by the Latest Thing and saith, "Wayne, thou son of thine absent father, fear not to let it be known on the manor that thou and Rubella art an item; for the sprog wot she's carryin' is from the Latest Thing. And it'll be a boy and thou shalt call his name BOSSY, for he shall save the People from their political-incorrectness."

Now all this was done, that it might be fulfilled, which was spoken of the Latest Thing by the New Age Guru, saying, "Behold, a single mother shall be up the duff, and shall bring forth a love child, and they shall call his name BOSSY, which, being interpreted is, 'Watch your back!'"

And Wayne, sobering up, like, did as the Vibe had bidden him and filled in the forms concerning him and Rubella demanded by the Social.

Still he wasn't knocking her off till she'd kittened: and he called his name BOSSY.

Now, when the Moderniser General was born in Islington, in the Great City, in the days of the Bureaucrat, behold there came non-discriminatory persons from the East End unto the street that is called Downing, saying, "Where is he (or she) that is born Facilitator of the People? For we read his (or her) horoscope in *The Star* and are come to check him (or her) out for compliance under the laws of health and safety."

When the Bureaucrat heard these things he was all, like, unglued, and all Downing Street with him.

And when he had gathered all the physicians of that which is called "spin", he enquired of them privily where the Moderniser General should be born.

And they say unto him, in Islington of the Great City: for thus it is written by the focus group, "And thou Islington in the land of Equal Opportunities art not least among the honchos of the People, for out of thee shall come a Chief Exec that shall rule in all the land called Nanny State."

Then the Bureaucrat, when he had called the non-discriminatory persons, enquired of them diligently what time the horoscope in *The Star* appeared. And they say unto him, "Lo, it appeareth in the colour supplement which is called *Naff* and followeth the section that is *Travel and Leisure*." He that hath ears to hear, let him hear.

And he sent them to Islington and saith, "Like, check it out then, and when thou hast found the kid, bring me an update that I may organise a photo-opportunity."

And when they had heard the Bureaucrat, they departed, and lo, *The Star* which they had read in the East End sent forth before them many scribes who stood over the place where the young kid was. And when they saw the Editor of *The Star*, they rejoiced with exceeding great joy.

And when they were come unto the tower block of the public housing unit – let him that readeth understand – they saw the kid with Rubella his mother, and fell down in the piss-soaked stairway and took many snaps of them on their digital cameras: and when they had opened their *Gucci* bags they brought forth gifts, alcopops, DVDs and *Viagra*.

And being warned of the *Daily Mail* astrologer, they departed into the East End by another way.

And being warned a second time by the Latest Thing on their mobiles, they departed into the East End on the 25 bus, for that lo, the Central Line was all screwed up as the custom is.

And when they were departed, behold, the Vibe of the Latest Thing appeareth to Wayne, rolling a joint, saying, "Arise and take the sprog and his mum and flee into Egypt."

And Wayne saith unto him, "Egypt – not bloody likely! There's all sand there and no human rights, and that!"

And, behold, the Vibe saith, "Well, get thee unto Neasden then. And be thou there until I bring thee word. For the Bureaucrat will seek the young sprog to ban him from the playgroup."

When he arose, he took the young sprog and his mum by night and departed even unto Neasden.

And he was there until the death of the Bureaucrat, that it might be fulfilled which was spoken of the Latest Thing by the Guru, saying, "Out of Neasden have I called my boy."

The Bureaucrat, when he saw that he was mocked of the non-discriminatory persons, was exceeding wroth, so that, as they say in their language, he went ballistic and banished all the young children in the Great City (from two years old and under) from the play-group, according to the time which he had diligently enquired of the non-discriminatory persons.

Then was fulfilled that which was spoken by the Guru, saying, "In the Great City was there a voice heard, lamentation and weeping and great mourning. Single mothers doing their nut because the kids were barred from the playgroup and they couldn't get no childcare while they sought to go forth on the piss."

But when the Bureaucrat was dead, behold, a Vibe from the Latest Thing appeareth unto Wayne, which was legless in Neasden, saying, "Sober up, man, and take the young sprog and his mum and go into the Great City, for they have lost the election which sought to ban the kid from the playgroup."

And he arose and took the young sprog and his mum and came even unto the Great City.

But when he heard that a new Bureaucrat did reign in that place, which cometh after the old Bureaucrat that was no more, he was afraid to go there: notwithstanding, being warned of the Archvibe in a nightdress, he turned aside into the parts of Essex.

And he came and dwelt in a city called Southend, that it might be fulfilled which was spoken by the Guru, "He shall be called a Sarfender."

CHAPTER II

And it came to pass in those days that there went out a decree from the Bureaucrat that the whole land should be overtaxed.

And all went to be overtaxed, everyone into his (or her) own city. And Wayne also went up from Essex, out of the city of Southend, unto the city of Dave (because he was of the house and lineage of Dave) to be overtaxed with Rubella his partner, being up the duff. And so it was that, while they were there, the days were accomplished that she should sprog.

And she brought forth her firstborn son, and wrapped him in a *Babygro* and laid him in that box the lager came in, for Wayne had pissed against the wall all the dosh she had saved for a pram.

And there were in the same county, estate agents abiding in the fields, keeping watch over land prices by night.

And lo, the Vibe of the Latest Thing came upon them and the buzz of the Latest Thing freaked them out and they were having kittens.

And the Vibe said unto them, "Have thee no kittens, for behold, I bring thee a brilliant news flash, which shall be to all People irrespective of race, creed, colour, sexual orientation or disability.

"For unto you is born this day in the city of Dave a Moderniser General which is called BOSSY, according to the promos and the long trailers for all this which thou hast no doubt seen on the telly.

"And this shall be a sign unto you, Ye shall find the sprog wrapped in a *Babygro*, lying in that cardboard box the lager came in."

And suddenly there were with the Vibe millions of Vibes of the Latest Thing, doing their nuts over the Latest Thing and saying: "Cheers to the Latest Thing, like altogether, man, and to the New Kid on the Block! Peacekeeping initiatives and equal opportunities (with social inclusion) among all People!"

And it came to pass as the Vibes were gone away from them into the www., the estate agents said to one another, "Let us go now even unto the Great City and see this thing which is come to pass, which the Latest Thing hath made known unto us."

And they came with haste and found Rubella his mother, and Wayne and the sprog, lying in a lager crate.

And when they had seen him, they blogged abroad the saying which was told them concerning this sprog. And all they that heard it were flipped out at these things that were spoken unto them by the estate agents.

But Rubella kept all these things up her jumper and said nowt to nobody.

And the estate agents returned, full of the Latest Thing and doing their nuts over all that had been spoken unto them of the Guru by the Vibes.

And when eight days were accomplished, behold, it was the Baby Welcoming Service – for in those days what was aforetime called the Christening had been done away with for its very discriminatoriness against the wog religions and offensiveness to them that didn't believe nuffin'. And Wayne had got loads of booze in to wet the sprog's head and lo, Wayne's dad (which is called in their language, Darren) took zillions of pics on his new mobile. And, behold, his name was called BOSSY, which was so named of the Vibe while Rubella was still up the duff.

And when the days were fulfilled that Rubella was fit to go out again, they brought him to the Great City to present him to the Latest Thing: as it is written in the database of the Guru, "Every male sprog from the time when its mum was first up the duff shall be called 'a very special baby' and its parent – or, if its dad hath done no runner, parents – shall arrange a photo-opportunity before the face of the Latest Thing.

And, behold, they shall bring unto the photo-opportunity of the store of their possessions, as it might be the old video recorder that they use no longer now they have got the DVD, or a few back issues of *Seventeen* or, if verily his father hath done no runner, some copies of *Nuts* also. Or it may be some other tits and bums mag like unto *Mayfair* or that which men call *Razzle*.

And lo, there was in those days a man in the Great City whose name was Kevin; and this man was a TV presenter for *The Latest Thing on Sunday Show*, even exceedingly compliant and Politically-Correct. And the Vibes were upon him. And the Vibes had revealed to him that in no wise would he be relocated until he had seen the Moderniser General.

And Kevin came by the Vibes into the studio and when Wayne and Rubella brought the young BOSSY in, as it was written in the database, he took the sprog in his arms and chucked him neath his chubby chin and saith,

"O Latest Thing, now lettest thou thy mediaguy depart in chuffedness, according to thy Guru. For mine eyes have shuftied thy lickspitter which thou hast prepared before the screens of all viewers, to be a celeb to fascinate the couch-potatoes and to be an icon for thy fan club on daytime TV."

And, behold, Wayne and Rubella were knocked out by these things that were said of him by the mediaguy.

And Kevin said, "Cheers! This child is set for the rising and falling of many in the ratings and he will be an icon in all the colour supplements – even in the supplement which is called *Naff*." And he saith to Rubella his mother, "Yea, a needle shall pierce thy belly-button and a tattoo shall be scratched by it, for a fashion statement to all the readers."

And there was one Anna, an astrological counsellor, which counselled by Tarot and Crystals for *Me Magazine*, the daughter of Trevor, the boss of *Slurp Productions PLC*. And verily Anna was old, even so old that she qualifieth for the bus pass. And this rumour was spread abroad of her throughout the land – that for all the seven years with her partner, he knocketh her not off.

Now she was a widow of fourscore years – and thou canst add on a few unto that – and in those days she departeth not from the TV studio neither by day nor by night and doth beseech the Latest Thing with mumblings and jabberings so that, if it had been possible, even the Latest Thing might weary of her.

And Anna, coming in that instant, likewise crieth "Cheers to the Latest Thing!" And she counselleth by the art of her counselling that BOSSY was to be the fab icon promised by all the Gurus, the Vibes and the Archvibes.

And lo, when all things concerning the photo-opportunity had been fulfilled, they returned unto Essex into their own city of

Southend. And the child grew – so that the neighbours said, "Surely he waxeth big for his age, and, behold, he hath all his chairs at home."

Now his parents went to the Great City every year on *Red Nose Day*. And when he was twelve years old, they went up to the Great City wearing their red noses withal. And when they had watched the humourless abasements until the time was fulfilled, they returned to Southend. But the child BOSSY tarried behind in the Great City and Rubella hadn't a sodding clue where he was.

But they, supposing him to have been on the bus, went as far as the M25, and they sought him among their kinsfolk and acquaintance. And, behold, all their kinsfolk and acquaintance were pissed, like.

And when they found him not, they turned back again to the Great City seeking him.

And it came to pass that, after three days, they found him in Broadcasting House, sitting in the midst of the BBC apparatchiks, both hearing them and asking them questions.

And all that heard him were astonished at his understanding and answers.

And when they saw him they went ballistic: and his mother said unto him, "You little bastard! What d'you think you're playing at? Behold, your dad and me's been, like, stressed out so you wouldn't believe."

And he said unto them, "Dost thou not believe? How is it that thou wast stressed out? Wist ye not that I must be getting myself clued up on the pinko lingo?"

And they understood not this saying which he spake unto them.

And he went down with them, even unto Southend and was grounded for three days. But his mother wouldn't let the matter drop. And BOSSY waxed bigger and smarter, the top kid on the block, even groomed for stardom according to the Latest Thing.

CHAPTER III

In those days cometh Jak the Aquatherapist, which did dip folk in the Serpentine, saying, "Change! Be positive and upbeat – for Cloud Cuckoo Land is at hand!"

For this is Jak that was spoken of by the Guru, saying, "The voice of one presenting in the area of natural beauty, 'Avail thyself of the Latest Thing. Make way for continuous change and development.'"

And this same Jak had his raiment a camel coat and a leather thong about his loins; and his wholefood diet was organic locusts and prime honey from selected hives. Then went out to him all the Great City and all the People along the banks of the Thames. And, behold, he did minister unto them with his aquatherapy in the Serpentine and did say unto them, "Go shopping – for the Latest Thing is at hand!" And they every one of them promised to chuck out all their old things and buy new things all the time.

But when he saw many of the Fogeys and Red Necks and them that were of the company which is called in their language Old Farts, he saith unto them, "O generation of has-beens! Who hath warned thee there be another promo on the way? Rend ye not your hearts but rend your garments and get ye to *Harvey Nicks* for some new gear.

"And think not to say we have plenty of nice pairs of flannels in the wardrobe and Harris tweed for our jackets, for I say unto you that the Latest Thing is able of these very special offers to raise up a whole new Lifestyle.

"For I indeed do render you aquatherapy unto energising, but he that cometh after me is more cutting-edge than I, whose flip-flops I am not worthy to wash off, and he will give unto thee the complete detox. For his aquatherapy is mightier than mine and he will give thee total infusion with the Spirit of the Age and special Javanese chilli powder."

Then cometh BOSSY from Southend unto Jak to be aquatherapised by him. But Jak forbade him, saying, "I have need to be detoxed by thee; and do thou come unto me for aquatherapy?"

But BOSSY, answering, saith, "Let it be for this promo, according to the script."

And BOSSY, when he was aquatherapised, went up straightway out of the water and, behold, the adverts came on and the music played and the Spirit of the Age descended upon him like it was wont to do on *Children in Need Day*. And lo, a voice from the producer's office, saying, "This is the Latest Thing On Earth. He's gonna make it – bigtime."

Then was BOSSY led by the Spirit of the Age into Medialand to be interviewed by an Agent. And when he had knocked around forty nights and slept for forty days, he was afterwards, like, peckish. And when the Agent came to him, he said, "If thou be the Guy with the Latest Thing, command that these empty fag packets be made *ciabatta*."

But he answereth and saith, "It is written, thou shalt not live by *ciabatta* alone, but by going up into *The Ivy* and even unto *Le Caprice* and partaking of the posh scoff that therein is."

Then the Agent taketh him into the City and setteth him on a window ledge up the Gherkin, and saith unto him, "If thou be the Guy with the Latest Thing, chuck thyself off. For verily I shall video thee on the way down and, behold, it looketh fab on the snuff movies."

And BOSSY saith unto him, "But verily that is not a trick thou canst do twice and I seek a longer career in showbiz."

Again, the Agent taketh him up an exceeding high tower block and sheweth him all the theatres and cinemas, pubs, clubs and revue bars and saith unto him, "Lo, I can make thee a star in all these joints if thou wilt pay unto me a commission of twenty-five per cent."

And he saith, "Look sonny, I'm the Latest Thing on Earth and I'm going solo. Sod thou off!"

Then the Agent soddeth off as was spoken of him by the mouth of BOSSY and, behold, he feeleth the force of the Vibes in that place.

And, leaving Southend, he came and dwelt in Shepherd's Bush, which is towards the West and handy for the Beeb, that it might be fulfilled which was spoken by the Guru, saying, "The People that sat in darkness in front of the telly have seen a great new series; and they that could aforetime receive only ITV have now got digital."

From that time BOSSY began his stand-up act and to say, "Wotcha cock – I'm the Latest Thing on Earth!"

And BOSSY, coming into the northern parts and walking by Camden Lock saw two guys, Simmy which was called Pete, and Andy, his mate, playing the one-armed bandits in the arcade, for verily they were the kids on the block. And straightway they left the bandits and followed him.

And going on from thence he seeth two other mates, Jim the son of Zeb, and Jon, his stepbrother by the new partner of his mother, with the which she was in an ongoing relationship. And they all immediately left their slot machines and became his groupies.

And BOSSY went about all their community centres promoting equal opportunities, non-discrimination and social inclusion according as he had been trained by the Latest Thing, and did preach the gospel of Political-Correctness and healed all manner of psychoneurosis among the malingerers. And his fame spread throughout all the City and they bring unto him all them that were taken with divers fashionable complaints, even with ME, post-traumatic stress disorder and Munchausen Syndrome by Proxy. And there followed him a great multitude of hangers-on and prurient sentimentalists from the City, from Shepherd's Bush and from all the region round about Essex.

And seeing the whole multitude of the great unwashed, he went up on to the Hill that is called Primrose, and when he was set his groupies came unto him. And he opened his mouth and gave them a presentation, saying,

"Chipper are the poor Millwall supporters, for they have been drawn against Arsenal.

"Chirpy are they that mourn, for they shall receive bereavement counselling.

"Ecstatic are the bashful, for they shall get assertiveness training.

"Buggered are they that do hunger and thirst after righteousness, for there's not much of that around these days.

"Right chuffed are the sentimental, for it's *Princess Di Day* next week.

"In luck are the impure of heart, 'cos there's lots of stuff for them on video and late-nite telly.

"Perky are they that belong to the peacekeeping process, for they shall share the loot with their brethren in the IRA.

"Frisky are they which are laughed at for Political-Correctness's sake, for they shall revise the compliance manual.

"Happy are ye, when Fogeys and Old Farts shall revile you and say all manner of racist and sexist things against you for my sake. Great is thy reward in Cloud Cuckoo Land, for so persecuted they the Gurus that were before you.

"Ye are the salt of the crisp packet, but if the salt produceth raised blood pressure then verily thou shalt take statins.

"Think not that I am come to destroy Standard Practice. I am come not to destroy but to fulfil. For verily I say unto you, Till Cloud Cuckoo Land and Medialand pass away, one jot or tittle shall in no wise pass from Standard Practice, till all be compliance.

"Whosoever therefore shall break one of these least footling proscriptions and shall teach his neighbour to say, 'Bollocks to Political-Correctness' shall be called the least in the Nanny State, and whosoever shall do and teach total compliance shall be greatest in the Nanny State.

"Ye have heard it was said of them in the old time, 'Thou shalt not kill. And whosoever shall kill shall be in danger of being strung up.' But I say unto you, whosoever shall kill shall be henceforth called a 'Victim' and 'Vulnerable' and shall receive psychotherapy. Verily I say unto you that his deed shall be set at nought. And the matter shall not be allowed to drop until all the psychiatric reports have been accepted.

"And whosoever shall say unto his colleague, 'Thou nerd or *schemiel* or pointy-head' shall be in danger of being monitored; but whoso calleth his colleague 'proper jerk' shall be in danger of social exclusion.

"Therefore if thou bring thy floral tribute to the roadside shrine at the end of thy neighbour's drive and there rememberest that thy colleague hath aught against thee, leave thy floral tribute by the roadside shrine, sign thee up for one of the conciliation courses according as the Compatibility Restoration Counsellor commandeth thee, then come and offer thy floral tribute at the roadside shrine which is at the end of the drive of thy neighbour.

"Seek compliance with him that is suing thee quickly while thou art on thy mobile to him, lest at any time he that is suing thee report thee to the Internal Examiner and the Internal Examiner deliver thee to the Medical Officer and the Medical Officer deliver thee to the Psychotherapist and the Psychotherapist to the funny farm. Verily thou shalt in no wise come out thence until all the psychiatric casework hath been fulfilled.

"Ye have heard that it was said by them of old time, 'Thou shalt not commit adultery', but I say unto you, 'Commit adultery as often as thou canst get thine end away, mate, for it is a liberated thing to put it around a bit, like. Only thou shalt wear a condom.'

"It hath been said, 'Whosoever shall put away his wife, let him give her a bill of divorcement.' But I say unto you that divorces, yea and even marriages, are but a small thing and to be taken up or set down as the whim taketh thee. It is good for men and women to enjoy many partners and verily to eschew all that monogamy and chauvinistic crap which were afore Modern Times.

"Again it hath been said, thou shalt not forswear thyself nor take the name of the Latest Thing in vain. But I say unto thee, that which was formerly abominable hath passed away, and now, as the custom is, they say 'fuck' every other word on the telly. Be fruitful and expostulate. Let thy 'arsehole' be thy 'arsehole' and thy 'bollocks' thy 'bollocks'.

"Ye have heard that it hath been said, 'An eye for an eye and a tooth for a tooth.' But I say unto you punishment is a very negative thing and part of the whole blame culture. Therefore, rather say I unto thee that, when offences come, thou shalt turn a blind eye. But whosoever smite thee on thy right cheek, thou mayest sue him in the small claims court for invading thy personal space.

"And whoso shall compel thee to go a kilometre, jog with him twain; for thus shall thy calories fall away and thy cholesterol be lowered. And the last state of that man is better than the first.

"But if a man ask of thee for thy cloak, tell him to get stuffed and go shopping for his own designer clobber at the *Nicks* which is called *Harvey* according as the Latest Thing hath commanded."

After saying these things, he departed from the region about the Hill that is Primrose and entered again into Essex.

CHAPTER IV

And he cometh into the house of Sim (which is called Pete) and Sim's mother lay sick with a fever. And Sim saith unto BOSSY, "Verily she is a right one for crogging it on and believeth now that she hath the 'flu which is called 'bird'."

And he went in unto the back bedroom wherein she sniffeth and wheezeth and he saith unto Sim, "She sulketh for thou makest the more fuss over me, thy new friend, than thou wast wont to make over her. Behold, it is called in the language of the physicians Attention-Seeking Syndrome, a disease psychosomatic."

And he took her by the hand and said unto her, "Woman, arise and be not grievously vexed with the Attention-Seeking Syndrome. I say unto thee, sulk thou not and even lighten up!"

And straightway the Attention-Seeking Syndrome left her and she did lighten up and maketh them all a cup of tea. And the People marvelled.

And at even, when the sun did set, there came unto him all the nutters and hysterics and malingerers, and his groupies said, "Tell them to sod off for, behold, they are a frigging nuisance."

And he saith, "Say not that they should sod off, neither are they a frigging nuisance. But behold, they suffer from that which is called Personality Disorder."

And he took one aside and saith, "Go show thyself unto the counsellor that counselleth for the Personality Disorder according as the Standard Practice commandeth thee."

And they did all go, and behold, they were every one of them lightened up and were no more vexed by the Personality Disorder.

Again he entered into the house and they bring one unto him that lieth on a bed, sick of the hangover, and they beseech him that he might heal him. BOSSY turneth to him that was sick of the hangover and saith, "Cheer up old son! Take thou the very hair of the dog."

But there were certain of the Fogeys and of the party which is called Old Farts and they say, "Behold, he goeth against Standard Practice for he commandeth this man to cheer up. And in no wise may a man be cheered up except it be by the Latest Thing."

And they all with one accord began to murmur against him and would feign have duffed him up.

But he, perceiving that which was in their hearts, saith, "Why reason ye these things in your hearts and why do ye say these things against me? For whether is it easier to say 'Cheer up!' or 'Arise, take up thy bed, get thee to the boozer and start getting pissed again'? But, that ye may know that the Son of Wayne hath power on earth to tell men to lighten up." He turned to the crashed-out alcy and saith, "Shift thyself matey, and see thou gettest out a bit more!"

And he that was the crashed-out alcy arose, took up his bed and belteth off downtown at a rate of knots, and lo, he cheereth up exceedingly and shaketh it all about as BOSSY had commanded him.

And they all marvelled, saying, "What manner of man is this that he telleth the attention-seekers to snap out of it and he that sulketh to cheer up, and even the miserable old gits obey him?"

And so he did sit down and eat with his groupies. And there came unto him all the disadvantaged and underprivileged of the inner city which were socially-excluded for to eat with him.

Now the Old Farts said unto the groupies, "How is it that he eateth with the disadvantaged and underprivileged and them that are socially-excluded and from the shitty end of town?"

When BOSSY heard it he was wroth and saith, "It is not the compliant which have need of the Standards Inspection Officer but they which are in breach of sections or subsections of the Manual of Procedure."

And no man any longer durst ask him any more damn fool questions.

And it came to pass that, as he walked with his groupies through the all-nite superstore on one of the *Diana Days*, and did eat some of the special choccies that no man might eat but were appointed to be set at one of the Di Shrines, they that were of the Old Farts said unto him, "Behold, why dost thou and thy groupies eat of the choccies which are appointed but for the Di Shrine to be set there for the Festival which is called 'Lachrymae'?"

But he saith unto them, "Have ye not heard what Dave did when he was peckish and fancied a bit of choccie – how he took the sacred Organic *Mars* Bar, and they that were with him, and did scoff until they damn near puketh?"

And they could not answer to him again to any of these things from out of their mouths. And they went their way.

In those days he passed through all the land of Essex and the country round about, teaching the gospel of Political-Correctness and delivering the People from all manner of imaginary diseases.

And when he drew nigh unto the Community Centre in the place that is called Basildon, they bring unto him one that was much lacking in the department which is called, in their language, gumption and as it saith in the Greek νους.

Certain of them say unto him, "This one is verily as thick as two short fucking planks."

And he answered them and said, "Sayest thou not that he is as thick as two short fucking planks, but that he hath learning difficulties. For lo, he is but two sandwiches short of the feeding of the five thousand."

And they say unto him, "But Functionary, he watcheth old Val Doonican videos and collecteth *Embassy* cigarette cards which were aforetime but are no more. Besides these things, behold, he singeth Shirley Bassey songs and offendeth against his neighbour. Surely he is as thick as two short fucking planks!"

He turneth unto him that hath the learning difficulties and saith, "What sayest thou concerning thy learning difficulties, for verily they that accuse thee declare thou art as thick as two short fucking planks? Dost thou know what thou sayest?"

And he crieth with a loud voice,
"Now Patrick McGinty, an Irishman of note
Fell in for a fortune and he bought himself a goat..."

And, behold, the Fogeys and they that were of the Old Farts party picked up stones wherewith to stone him. Yet holdeth he not his tongue, but cried out all the more in the manner of the Doonican that is called Val,
"Says he, sure of goat's milk I'm goin' to have me fill
But when he brought a Nanny home, he found it was a Bill..."

And BOSSY saith unto his groupies, "You were right. He is as thick as two short fucking planks!" And he put his fingers over his mouth and saith, "Peace! Be still! And cry no more of the Doonican that is called Val, neither of that Paddy McGinty; and let not the gender of the goat be so much as mentioned among you. But be thou delivered of thy learning difficulties and be no more fucking plankish."

And straightway he held his tongue and arose and took himself to the Enrolling Officer and the Enrolling Officer enrolled him in the Southend University, and he taketh his degree in Media Studies with Golf and Ten-Pin Bowling.

And the Fogeys departed with them that were of the Old Farts party and returned to their own place. But the People marvelled, saying, "He hath done all things well. He maketh him that hath the learning difficulties to have no more the learning difficulties; and behold, the two short fucking planks are not fucking short with him."

CHAPTER V

And when his groupies had gathered round, he spake unto them in his doctrine and said, "When thou givest thine alms be certain that thou makest a song and dance about it, even a huge ballyhoo. Ye have heard it said, 'Do thy goodness by stealth and let no man see what thou doest.'

"But I say unto you, when thou doest aught for charity, shout it from the housetops. And if it so be that it is *Red Nose Day*, then put on thy red nose. And if it be *Children in Need*, then take thee to the humourless abasements and feign to have a good time. And on *World AIDS Day*, wear thy condom openly, that all may see it and rejoice that thou expressest solidarity with them that have fallen sick from their too much batting for the other side, and that which is called in their language 'the rear-entry method'. She that hath ears to hear, let her hear.

"Ye have heard it said aforetime, 'Cursed is he that lieth with his brother and all them that do bat for the other side.'

"But I say unto thee, be thou Gay, put on thy condom and thy earring, and if thou art well in the way in the riches of this world, thy designer leathers and thy shirt which is called polo-neck and finest cashmere. And paint thy face, get thee a float and mince along the street that is called Strand. Preach the gospel of puffiness to all People. And they that will not go with thee and take up the rear-entry method, let them be called Homophobes.

"Hast thou not heard what he that is called Touchy Tatch did when he perceiveth that the Chief Fogey condemneth the rear-entry method – how he ascendeth even unto the pulpit of the Chief Fogey, as the Chief Fogey speaketh long to all the Old Farts, and saith unto him that verily he was an Homophobe?"

And they all begin to say unto him, "Chair, teach us of the Latest Thing and how we might draw nigh unto the Latest Thing."

He saith unto them, "Thou shall love the Latest Thing with all thy heart, with all thy soul and with all thy strength, and thyself before thy neighbour.

"And when ye pray, take thee to the midst of the assembly, jig about a bit, like; and wave thine arms so that they say, 'Behold, he hath the learning difficulties'; and even the Fogeys, the Old Farts and the politically-incorrect do say, 'Verily he's a frigging loony!'

"And in that which is called among them 'The Peace', do thou fawn on thy neighbour and make abundant greeting and kiss him or her with great zeal, so that the Fogeys do ask, 'Is he trying to score with that bird, or what?'

"And when thou prayest be not as the Fogeys are, which make vain repetitions from books which are old and make those petitions which were spoken of them in the old time. For they do say, 'O Lord, our heavenly Father, high and mighty King of kings, Lord of lords, the only ruler of princes...' and other such things which be an abomination to the Latest Thing. Verily I say unto thee, they have their reward.

"But when thou prayest, let thy praying be from the book that is modernised and which payeth not regard for those things that are discriminatory on grounds of gender, race and class. Let thy petitions be for them that are called underprivileged, disadvantaged and vulnerable – and whatsoever the new buzz phrase is for them that are flavour of the month, do thou pray for them, as it happeneth asylum seekers or them that are transgendered or the insurgent which doth insurge against thy People in a strange land.

"And afterward take thee for Fair Trade coffee and devour thee plentifully of the biscuits that are from shitty countries and that taste even very shitty. Remember, when thou prayest, that thou use the guitar abundantly. And seek out for her that prayeth the fat woman with the voice that be exceeding sanctimonious and she that doth cover her face with all manner of adornment so that the People say, 'Blimey, someone's given her a right paint job!'

"And when thou prayest, behold, make thee long prayers, even prayers that are very long; and faint not when the Fogeys shall say, 'Bloody hell, she goeth on a bit!' Neither when they that are of the Old Farts party say, 'Fancy coming to church in a skirt like that! Behold, thou couldst see her very arse.'

"And do thou make sure thou hast switched on the microphones, that thou mayest be heard of women and men to pray. And when thy prayer is heard among women and men, thou shalt receive a round of applause according to the Latest Thing.

"After this manner therefore pray,

'O Latest Thing
Which art to die for,
Funky be thy name.
Thy newness come,
Thy cutting edge done
In our Lifestyle
As it is on the telly.
Give us this day our daily fix
And forgive us our political-incorrectness
But we don't forgive them that are politically-incorrect
    against us.
Lead us into temptation
And deliver us from boredom,
For thine is the attitude,

The modernisation and the entertainment
Twenty-four seven
A-person.'

"Moreover when thou goest forth on the binge, adorn thyself in thy best clobber and anoint thyself with the unguents, perfumes and costly lotions that thou seest advertised in the supplements which are coloured, that they which see thee binge may know for a surety that thou art on the binge. And, behold, divers of these lotions do attract the birds like there's no tomorrow, like; even as it is said of them, 'they panteth for it'.

"Thou shalt not anoint thyself with the balm that is called in their language *Old Spice*, the balm that is used of the Fogeys. Verily they have their reward.

"Lay up treasures for thyself in equities and bonds where neither moth nor rust doth corrupt and where thieves do not break through and steal. For where thy treasure is, there shall thy Lifestyle be also.

"And see that thou dost indeed serve two masters, for when thou pleasest the one thou shalt please the other also. Thou canst easily serve the Latest Thing and Lifestyle.

"Take thee thought for thy life, what thou shalt eat and what thou shalt drink, and the designer clobber that thou shalt put on. For is not Lifestyle altogether that thou consumest? And, behold, the tills they rattle throughout the shopping precincts.

"Consider Lily, who hath that nice little boutique by St Martin-in-the-Fields, and even the birds of the catwalk, for they take thought by day and by night what they shall put on, and verily the Latest Thing becometh them. And lo, the Solomon Grundies in all their fogeyness are not arrayed like *Roberto Cavalli*.

"Wherefore if the Latest Thing so clothe the underprivileged and disadvantaged and even the Chavs from the inner city with pirated designer labels from off the peg, how much niftier shalt thou be clothed, O ye of loadsamoney?

"And take thee thought of the morrow, where thou shalt binge and whom thou shalt screw. 'Cos it's important to have these things worked out aforehand, like.

"Judge and thou shalt be judged, for hath not the Latest Thing decreed that behold, Lifestyle is a beauty contest?

"And why beholdest thou the mascara that doth adorn thy sister's eye? Thou airhead! First use thine own proprietary cleansing cream as it commandeth thee in the supplements, then thou shalt see clearly to remove the mascara that is thy sister's.

"Give not that which is new and cool to the dogs which do hang about the disco, neither cast thou thy pearls before the swine that would tear them from thy neck on thy way back from the Ladies.

"Ask, and it shall be given thee – if thou nag and pester long enough. Seek and thou shalt find. And if thou seekest and findest not, then, behold, thou shalt chuck it and buy another one.

"Therefore, whosoever hearkeneth unto these promos of mine and the fashion statements that I have spoken unto thee, he is like one who purchased a house in Islington and, behold, when the property prices went through the roof, he maketh a killing and saith, 'I'm all right, mate. I bought at the right time!' And he moveth even unto Chelsea.

"But to him that getteth him a house in Chelsea when prices are at an all-time high, then I say unto him, 'Thou fool!' And the last state of that man is worse than the first."

CHAPTER VI

And the third day there was a celebration of a civil partnership in Soho and BOSSY's old lady was there. And both BOSSY was called and his groupies to the piss-up.

And when they wanted some more of that strong cider, the old lady of BOSSY saith unto him, "They've none of that strong cider."

BOSSY saith unto her, "Old lady, why givest thou me grief? S'not as if it's my fault is it? I'm only here for that thou demandest of me that I come to the piss-up of the civil partnership of thy puffy friends Jeremy and Jamie."

His old lady saith unto the caterers, "Whatsoever he saith unto you, do it."

And there were set there six canisters of plastic after the manner of the non-drinking of the *Alcoholics Anonymous*, containing thirty or forty gallons apiece.

BOSSY saith unto them, "Fill the canisters with water."

And they filled them to the brim.

And he saith unto them, "Draw out now and bear unto the guvnor." And they bear it.

When the guvnor of the piss-up had tasted the water that was made strong cider, and knew not whence it was, but the flunkeys which drew the water knew, the guvnor of the piss-up calleth one of the Gay couple and saith unto him,

"Every guy at the beginning doth set forth great booze, and when everyone falleth about pissed, like, then cometh the crappy two per cent by volume rubbish which dunt do nuffin' for nobody, like. But thou hast saved the lulu juice until now!"

This beginning of promos did BOSSY in Soho of the Great City, and manifested forth his coolness. And his groupies thought he was the Latest Thing.

And, behold, they went from thence unto the country of them that speak in the language of Estuary which is over against Essex towards the forest. And there met him out of the town a certain guy which was grievously tormented. He wore no clothes, neither abode in any house but ran about the municipal cemetery.

And one of his groupies, called Bart, began to ask him, saying, "What's up with him then? He looks bloody crackers to me."

And BOSSY was much displeased and answereth them, saying, "Say not that he is bloody crackers. Say rather that he hath the bipolar disorder which in the time of their political-incorrectness they were wont to call the manic-depressive psychosis."

And when he that hath the bipolar disorder seeth BOSSY he cried out with a loud voice and fell down before him, saying, "Keep thine hands off me, thou BOSSY, son of the Latest Thing. Don't come near me with thy therapy and thy counselling!"

(For BOSSY had commanded the bipolar disorder to come out of the man. For oftentimes it had caught him so that he was tagged by order of the Bureaucrat. And he chucketh away the tagging wherewith he was tagged and was driven of the bipolar disorder into the cemetery.)

And BOSSY asked him, "What is thy name?"

And he answereth, "Legion, for we are many."

And Bart turned unto BOSSY and saith, "Sodding hell! It soundeth more like schizophrenia than bipolar disease to me."

And BOSSY saith, "Thou hast spoken well, Bart. We'll make a doctor of thee yet – just like thine uncle Luke."

So he calleth the multitudinous schizophrenic abnormal personality manifestations divers long names in the Latin tongue. And one of them cried in a loud voice, "See that thou chuckest us not into the lake, we beseech thee! For we swim not."

And Jon saith unto BOSSY, "See – I told thee he wast bloody crackers!" And, behold, he smirketh.

But BOSSY turneth unto him and saith, "Smirk thou not. But that thou may know that the Latest Thing on Earth hath power to apply the correct therapy to both the bipolar disease and to the schizophrenia –" He turneth to the sodding loony and crieth, "Get thee into yonder load of pigs!"

And the loony was wroth and saith, "What meanest thou, get thee into the pigs, Guv? I might be a sodding loony but verily I'm no pig-shagger!"

Nevertheless he saith, "Again I say unto thee, Get thee into the pigs!"

Then went the bipolar disorder – or as it might be the multitudinous schizophrenic abnormal personality manifestations or even the bloody crackers-ness – out of the man and into the pigs which ran violently down a deep place into the lake and were drowned.

When they that fed the pigs, and whose the pigs were saw what was done, they spake unto BOSSY and his groupies with many words, so that verily the air waxed blue. And they call the RSPCA Inspection Officers. And the RSPCA Inspection Officers call the Animal Rights fanatics and the groupies were sore afraid.

But BOSSY saith unto his groupies, "Be ye not affrighted, for behold, if I hear another peep out of these Animal Rights fanatics, I'll chuck them into the lake after the pigs."

Then a great fear came upon the Animal Rights fanatics and them that were of the RSPCA Inspection Office and they scarpereth. And the groupies did laugh them to scorn and Pete putteth forth his tongue and saith, "Ner-ner, Ne-ne-ner-ner-ner! That's got you bastards, annit?"

But afterward, Bart taketh BOSSY apart and saith unto him, "Why doest thou that, then? Why sendest thou the pigs into the lake so that they are altogether perished out of the land? For we thought that thou wast he that wast in all things Politically-Correct, and that thou comest out to teach men the gospel of Political-Correctness."

And BOSSY saith unto him, "Oh I dunno, Bart. Sometimes you just think you've gotta go for it!"

And they all begin to say with one voice, "Ah, BOSSY, thou art a Right One!" And they call him "a proper card" and other such things as men say when they know in their hearts that this is the Gaffer.

And they departed out of the jurisdiction of the RSPCA Inspectors. And a great fear came upon all the Animal Rights fanatics and they say, "We had thought BOSSY should be the one to teach us Political-Correctness in all things, but lo, he hath killed our pigs."

Others said, "Fret not, for it is his custom to teach the Political-Correctness. Behold, he wast stressed out and throweth a wobbly."

And they all with one accord call after him and say, "O Facilitator, do thou throw no more the wobbly and return ye not to our coasts!"

Then came to him his mother and his brethren, for of a truth he hath brethren by this time, for Wayne keepeth not his hands off Rubella so that it was said of her by her neighbours, "Behold, she's always up the duff, that one. Like unto rabbits they are, 'er and that Wayne." And they say again, "Like unto rabbits!"

And, behold, his mother and brethren could not get near him for the *paparazzi*. And it was told him by certain of the *paparazzi* which said, "Thy mother and thy brethren stand without, desiring to see thee."

And he saith unto them, "Without what?"

And they say, "Without a clue. Well, you know what they're like – behold, they are, like, six firkins short of a miraculous piss-up."

And he saith, "Who is my mother? Who are my brethren? Verily I say unto you, they that loveth the Latest Thing – they are my mother and my brethren."

Now it came to pass on the following Wednesday that he went into a ship with his groupies, for he saith unto them, "Behold, I am desirous of checking the water for sodium content and even for nitrates that it be pure enough for the hypochondriacs in that which is called of them the Green Party to drink."

And they launched forth.

But as they sailed, he fell asleep and there came down a storm of wind over the lake and the ship was filled with water. And they were sore afraid, even so sore that they shit themselves. And that maketh them the more sore.

And they come to him and say, "Facilitator, Facilitator, we perish and lo, yet afore we perish we do shit ourselves!"

But he arose from sleep and saith, "Shit not yourselves for this verily is the manner of tempest that ye should look for in the days of the Global Warming. As it was foretold by the Green Guru where he saith:

'Behold, the days come, when the cattle shall fart exceedingly and the chimneys shall smoke and the air shall be filled with greenhouse gases. And there shall be wailing and gnashing of teeth. And lo, it pisseth down a whole lot more than it was accustomed to in the old times.'"

And he rebuketh the Global Warming and of a sudden there was a great calm. And his groupies wondered and began to say among themselves, "Who is this that even the greenhouse gases do obey him?"

CHAPTER VII

And when he was come down from the mountain, great multitudes followed him. And, behold, there came a man grievously vexed with the *acne vulgaris,* which is called in their language pimples. And he worshipped him, saying, "Facilitator, if thou wilt thou canst make me clean of the pimples which are called pimples."

And BOSSY had compassion upon the man that had the *acne vulgaris* for he perceiveth that it put the birds off no end. And he saith, "God, you look a proper sight!"

And he put forth his hand and touched him, saying, "Yuk, it's all, like, lumpy and that, innit? I can't do nothing about it, but get thee the health and beauty supplement and do buy for thyself the incredibly costly face cream advertised therein.

"And get thee to the disfigurement counsellor and offer thy first instalment in the easy-pay therapy course for the aesthetically challenged, as the health and beauty supplement commandeth thee."

And immediately he went forth unto the paper shop. And his groupies marvelled, seeing that such power was given unto men that he was able to send pock-marked pillocks to the newsagents.

And when BOSSY was entered into Islington, behold, there came unto him a peace activist beseeching him, saying, "My servant lieth at home, differently-abled, grievously tormented."

But when he heard this saying, BOSSY was wroth and rent his garment and saith unto the peace activist, "What is this that thou sayest, 'my servant'? Hast thou not heard of the Equal Opportunities Commission and the law which saith thou shalt not discriminate on the grounds of race, creed or class? How is it that thou hast a servant?"

And he could not answer him to any of these things.

And BOSSY waxed exceeding wroth and saith unto him that hath the servant, "Come on now – thou hast a tongue in thine head. Answer thou me and keep not silence."

And he saith, "Facilitator, thou hast well spoken. Let him be no more my servant but my friend." And he fell at his feet and wept.

When he saw the things which had come to pass, Pete saith, "Look at that will you, boys – another freaking sentimentalist!"

And the peace activist denieth not, but confessed and said, "Facilitator, I am not worthy that thou shouldst come into my Pacifist Campaign HQ, but speak the word only and my servant – sorry, he that aforetime was my servant but that is verily now my friend – shall be healed."

The groupies begin to say, "Just hearken at him crogging it on. Talk about flannel!"

And the peace activist holdeth not his tongue, but confesseth openly, "For I am a man under authority, having peaceniks, CND members and other useful idiots under me. And I say to this person 'Go' and she goeth; and to another, 'Come' and she cometh; and to my servant – sorry, to the one that was aforetime my servant – 'Do this' and he doeth it."

And the Moderniser General turneth to his groupies and saith, "Hearken at all that! And I thought it was I that was called BOSSY!"

And his groupies laughed so that they piss themselves.

And BOSSY saith unto him that besought him, "Just have another go at framing thy request, sonny, and I'll see what I can do."

And when he had come to his right mind he beginneth again to ask for him that was aforetime his servant but was now called his friend, "For I am a man of equal opportunities and non-elitist. I beseech thee to heal him that is differently-abled."

And BOSSY saith, "Ah, but not sick of the palsy, is he? Tell you what, mate, we're all bloody sick of the palsy! What man among you isn't sick of the palsy?"

And, behold, his groupies do wet themselves the second time.

And BOSSY turneth to him that besought him and saith, "Go thy way. As thou hast spoken so shall it be done unto thee. Though I have not heard such bullshit – no, not in all Islington and Camden."

When the even was come they brought unto him many that were possessed with learning difficulties, and behold, he did cast out the learning difficulties and did write sick notes for all them that were desirous to be signed off on the sick, even them which suffered that which in the Latin tongue is called *oscillatio plumbi*.

Now when they see great multitudes coming upon them, the groupies gave commandment in his name, saying, "Piss ye off to the other side!"

And they all every one of them pissed off, saying, "He hath done all things well. He both signeth the sick notes for the malingerers and casteth out the learning difficulties. And, behold, he saith to this man, 'Piss off!' and straightway he pisseth off."

And a certain hack from *The Star* cometh unto him and saith, "Facilitator, I will be thy groupie and follow thee whithersoever thou goest and write about thy doings in the supplement that is called *Naff*."

And he saith unto him, "So? I've got plenty of groupies already. Lo, the foxes have a hunting ban and the birds of the air are protected by the commissars in the RSPB; but the Guy with the Latest Thing hath not where to lay his head."

And another wannabe groupie saith, "Suffer me first to go and bury my father."

And, behold, his groupies watched him to see what he would do.

BOSSY answereth him and saith, "Let the *Co-op Mortician Service* bury thy father, for thou canst claim it back on the Social. Do thou follow me!"

And the whole company wondered at his saying and understood not the saying which he saith, and behold, it was hid from them. And the multitudes departed unto the posh shops.

Then was brought unto him one possessed of a spirit of sulkiness, griping and mooning and of great grumpiness. And he taketh him by the hand and commandeth the spirit of negativity and down-beatness to come out of him.

And straightway he falleth about with the giggles and his grin was even like unto the banana split. And BOSSY saith unto him, "Get thee on the *Radio Two* phone-in that all People might hear how thou hast cast away thy down-beatness and displayest the vacuous frivolity which belongeth to all them that are possessed of the Latest Thing."

And straightway he that was healed of the spirit of grumpiness, lowereth his trousers and flasheth his very arse at them which drew nigh. And when they saw this, they did laugh and one came forth and said, "Verily thou art good enough for that thine appearance may be on the show that is called *I'm A Celebrity: Get Me Out of Egypt* as it is written."

But they all with one voice say unto him, "Why forgettest thou, that which was aforetime Egypt is now Neasden – for remember how it was said of him, 'Egypt – not bloody likely! There's all sand there and no human rights, and that!'"

And lo, they all fell about in the spirit of vacuous frivolity as the custom is.

Now when the spirit of grumpiness had come out of the man, the Fogeys and they that were of the Old Farts drew near to him and said, "Thou castest out grumpiness by Old Grumpy, the spirit of grumpiness."

But he saith, "If I by Old Grumpy cast out grumpiness, by whom do thy lot cast it out?"

(For he knew whereof he spoke, and that the Old Farts and the Fogeys cast not out the spirit of grumpiness but follow that spirit and are led by it all the days of their lives.)

And they could not answer him to any of these things.

Now the Old Farts were exceeding grumpy and down-beat and weary of all the humourless abasements and the modernisation that was throughout all the land. They were even like unto the Fogeys which loved not the colour supplements which are called *Naff*, and did abhor the music which is Rap and Rock and soundeth out through all the air and ceaseth not by day, and in the night-season giveth no rest.

And BOSSY said, "When the spirit of grumpiness is gone out of a person, he walketh through dry places seeking rest and, finding none (save only in the exceeding grumpiness that is called the *Carlton Club*. She that hath ears to hear, let her hear), he saith, 'I will return unto the miserable bugger from whence I came out.'

"And when he returneth, he findeth him that was formerly called miserable bugger all washed out – for he hath since the day of his deliverance clubbed exceedingly even that he was all binged out, like.

"Then the spirit of grumpiness goeth and findeth seven other spirits more grumpy than himself and they enter into the miserable bugger. And the last state of that miserable bugger is grumpier than the first."

And he calleth to him all the Fogeys and the Old Farts and saith unto them, "All manner of political-incorrectness and down-beatness and elitism shall be forgiven. But there remaineth one offence for which there is no forgiveness. Cursed therefore is he that shall offend against the Spirit of the Age."

CHAPTER VIII

Now when Jak the Aquatherapist heard in the care-in-the-community home the works of BOSSY, he sent two of his physios which said unto him, "Art thou he that should come, or look we for another?"

BOSSY answered and said unto them, "The visually-challenged are wearing strong glasses and the hearing-impaired have their hearing aids. The pimpled are de-pimpled, the semi-comatose malingerers are raised up and the underprivileged and disadvantaged have the gospel of Political-Correctness preached unto them. And chirpy is he whosoever will not get stroppy with me."

And as they departed, BOSSY began to say unto the multitudes concerning Jak, "What went ye out to the Serpentine for to see – a toff clothed in a stripy suit? Behold, they that wear stripy suits are in the *Carlton Club*. But what went ye out for to see – a Guru? Yea, I say unto thee, and more than a Guru, for this is he of whom it saith in all the promos and trailers, 'Behold, I send my warm-up man before thy face which shall prepare the audience before thou comest on.'

"Verily I say unto thee, among them that have ministered the therapy which is called 'alternative', there hath not risen a greater than Jak.

"But whereunto shall I liken this generation? It is like unto children sitting in the amusement arcades and calling to their mates, 'We gave you the *iPod* but you would not dance. We gave you some charlie, but ye would not snort.'

"For Jak came neither dancing nor snorting and they say he hath the spirit of grumpiness. But the Guy with the Latest Thing came dancing and snorting and thou sayest, 'Behold, a piss-artist utterly arseholed, a mate of publicans and twenty-four hour boozing!'"

At that time the Bureaucrat heard of the fame of BOSSY and was wroth. And he calleth his apparatchiks and saith, "This is Jak the Aquatherapist returned from the Special Needs Unit!"

For the Bureaucrat had lain hold on Jak and taken him unto the care-in-the-community home and to keep him under observation there. (For behold, his brother Philip's wife, Fukme, was pissed off with him. For Jak hath said that verily the Bureaucrat might not knock her off, for their Chi energies were incompatible and even their Yin and Yang were, like, out of synch.)

And, behold, the wife of the Bureaucrat was a victim of the psychopathic syndrome. But others say, "Sod that – she's a mean cow and a raving nutter!"

Now when the Bureaucrat's birthday was kept, Polony, the daughter of Fukme – she of the cleavage like unto the Cave of Machpelah – danced before them and pleased the Bureaucrat. So that the Bureaucrat did promise with an oath, saying, "Bloody hell! Look at the tits on yon bint!" to give her whatsoever she wouldst, up to the half of all the houses and lands which were given unto him by the tycoons according to what is called "sweeteners".

And Polony, being instructed of Fukme her mother, saith, "Give me the dick of Jak the Aquatherapist as a hot dog."

And when he heard this the Bureaucrat was bummed out. Nevertheless, for his oath's sake and for the sake of them that sat in the disco with him, he commanded that it be given her even as she had required him.

And he sent and de-dicked Jak the Aquatherapist in the Special Needs Unit. And his dick was brought in a takeaway carton and given unto Polony who lay it before Fukme, her mother.

And Polony saith unto her, "Fukme, it doth appear like unto a Frankfurter!"

Then cometh Jak's groupies and take up his dickless body and bring it even unto Golders Green crematorium. And they tell BOSSY of all these things that had come to pass at the Birthday Disco of the Bureaucrat. When BOSSY heard of it, he departed thence into the country round about Dagenham.

And when he had called unto him the twelve groupies, he gave them skills against the psychoneuroses, the fashionable ailments and all manner of imaginary diseases among the People: the *acne vulgaris* (which hath aforetime been called pimples), the ME and the post-traumatic stress disorder, the Munchausen Syndrome by Proxy, the Narcissistic Personality Disorder, spurious allergic reactions, *anorexia nervosa* (which is called in their language "the attention-seeking throwing-up syndrome"), sundry forms of malingering and divers kinds of "stress".

Now the names of the twelve are these: the first Sim (or Simmy) which is called Pete; Andy his brother; Jim the son of Zeb; and Jon (not the Aquatherapist); Phil, Bart, Tom and Matty the VAT man; Jim the son of Alf (which in the days of their political-incorrectness was called "the cripple"); Jude the brother of Jim, which is called "Hey Jude"; Simon the pufta; Jude the Fogey, which betrayed him. There were also among his groupies a great many sheilas and chief among them she that was called Mad Magda. Moreover, every one of them was what was formerly called "a wog".

All these he appointeth for to bear witness that he chooseth his groupies irrespective of race, gender, sexual orientation or disability.

These twelve BOSSY sent forth and commanded them, saying, "Go not into Scotland, nor into that country wherein are they that are called 'Taffs'; but go ye rather to the politically-incorrect of the nation that is England.

"And as ye go say, 'Behold, Cloud Cuckoo Land is at hand with all manner of modernisation.'

"Counsel the neurotic, cleanse their pimples, humour the suggestible, raise them that have the hysterical paralysis (which were formerly the malingerers) and cast out the psychoneuroses and all manner of dietary and health fads. And in all these things see ye that ye pay due and honourable service to Quality Assurance and all manner of Compliance.

"Take neither purse nor scrip, neither any credit card, ready or cheque book; for behold, there is a rich living to be made out of the suckers which pay for all this attention.

"And into any health department ye enter, enquire of him or her that is called Head of Centre, and abide with him or her until ye go hence.

"And when ye come into an house, disinfect it and see ye do the Feng Shui according to the word that was spoken unto you by the Gurus. And whosoever shall not pay thee for thy therapy, thy counselling and thy Feng Shui, tell them that verily they get not this sort of treatment on the NHS.

"Behold, I send you forth as caring agents among the stiff upper lips. Be ye therefore as skilled as stress counsellors and as euphemistic as psychotherapists.

"But beware of Fogeys and them that be not modernised. For they will mock you and tell jokes about you in bad taste. They will deliver thee up to their pubs and clubs, and finally they will set thee at nought and satirise thee.

"But when they bring you into their pubs and clubs for to mock you, take no thought for what ye shall say, for lo, the Latest Thing shall give you utterance and ye shall answer them unto their mockery and their satirising out of the Standard Practice, the Manual of Compliance and the Laws of Political-Correctness which shall never be removed."

And he saith unto them in his doctrine, "Are not two sparrows protected by the RSPB? Ye are of more value than many sparrows – and here's the Certification of Competence to prove it.

"Whoso therefore shall be a groupie of mine, he shall be also a groupie of the Latest Thing. For the Latest Thing and I are an item. But whosoever shall not do as the Latest Thing commandeth, shall feel a right Charlie when the Latest Thing doth appear in all its glory.

"For I am come to set a man at variance against his father, and the daughter against her mother. And thine enemies shall be thine own household. And any child that loveth his or her father and mother more than he or she loveth Complete Compliance, shall be removed from thence. And, behold, I send before thee Social Workers and divers of that which is called 'Inspectorate', and they shall take thee from that place unto a place of Political-Correctness as the Standard Practice hath commanded them.

"And verily father shall be set against son, and daughter against her mother until that Day of the Latest Thing cometh and modernisation be accomplished over the whole land."

CHAPTER IX

And it came to pass that he sent the multitudes away and constrained his groupies to get into a boat and go before him unto the other side, peradventure he would come upon them ere the sun was risen.

But when the ship was now in the midst of the lake, it was tossed with waves, for the wind was contrary.

And, behold, he came unto them walking on the water.

When the groupies saw him walking on the water, they were freaked out and some they kitteneth and Bart saith, "It's a ghost – like unto that one we watched in that movie in Southend, *The Lady in White*. Remember ye it?"

And Matt saith, "Thou meanest that movie with the damsel that is called Sharon Stone, wherein she crosseth and uncrosseth her legs, and verily we get an eyeful of her – "

"Of a surety it was not that movie, for that was called *Basic Instinct* and I do believe it also starred Michael Douglas and the damsel Stone hath said, when the movie was ended, that verily the scenes of lust be so marvellous in their configuration that she and Douglas were 'the horizontal Fred and Ginger of the 1990s'. And lo, there appeareth no spook in it."

Whereupon, Pete was wroth and greatly angered and saith, "Cut the crap ye two! For it appeareth like unto BOSSY which walketh on the water."

And BOSSY calleth to them, saying, "Be thou not freaked out, for it is I! Behold my new act which I do prepare that the multitudes might go, 'Ooh!' for they believe it happeneth some great sign and wonder. But the great number of Scribes and Interpreters that be of the Deconstructionist Party which come after shall say, 'Think not that this be a sign, but a pericope of the salvific narrative and verily no more than *une parole* in the *langue* which is called *mythos*."

And Pete crieth out in a loud voice and saith, "Facilitator, I would be of thy pericope and thy salvific narrative which they that be of the Deconstructionist Party do preach. For lo, I have made long reading of the *Gesamtkrisistheologie* in the scroll that is *Wissenschaft für Einen Neuen Zeitgeist* that even I also might bore the very arse off any of them that listen."

And straightway, Pete jumpeth over the side and floundereth.

And they all with one voice begin to call out, "He's fallen in the wa-ter!" And do laugh him to scorn.

But BOSSY upbraided them for their hardness of heart and taketh Pete by the hand and raiseth him up, saying, "Thou wilt have to practise a lot more, lad, before thou canst enter this pericope. For this Deconstruction cometh only after much of that which is called 'smoke and mirrors'."

And the multitudes which were afar off and they that were nigh gave unto both BOSSY and Pete the big hand and cry out that they do likewise and a second time also.

And in the morning when they were set, behold, his groupies come unto him and say, "Moderniser General, open our eyes that we may see the mysteries of that which is called 'Deconstruction' and the doctrine thereof that, seeing, we might understand all the mysteries of the *Wissenschaft für Einen Neuen Zeitgeist*."

But he saith, "Unto them that are without it is not given to understand the Deconstruction neither the bum-clenching circumlocution and reductive egocentric hermeneutics of their *Lebensformen*. But unto you it shall be made known."

And they did roll them their joints, for there was much grass in the place.

And he saith unto them concerning the Deconstruction, "Verily it followeth after the *Logiksprache* of him that was called Gottlob Frege, only that there be the eternal cross-referencing of that which is *Sinn* but there be no *Bedeutung*."

Pete saith unto him, "Thou meanest there be everlasting shades of interpretation but no ontological substratum of which the interpretation be the interpretation."

When he had spoken these things, behold, BOSSY looked on him and wondered. And he saith, "Verily it be with the Deconstruction even as thou hast said. It is a load of crap."

And they all say, "Now thou speakest not in that which is of the salvific narrative, neither the metonymical utterance. Now thou speakest plain and we know for a surety that the demythologising *Kritiksmethodologie* is crap."

And lo, he turneth to Pete and, like, chucked him under the chin.

In those days he began to speak to them in riddles and they beseech him, "Tell us what meaneth thy riddles for the secret of their words is hid from us, neither understand we thy jargon."

"No problem," he saith.

"Hear ye therefore the spin of the sower. The sower is the Guru or it happeneth the counsellor or even him which is called therapist or the physician of that which is called 'spin' who serveth the Bureaucrat.

"When anyone heareth the modern message, that which belongeth to Cloud Cuckoo Land or which telleth of the perfect life for all People which shall be delivered by the Bureaucrat, the Chief Fogey cometh and saith that, behold, the promo is but bullshit and that all the modernising initiatives be but crap, this is the seed that fell by the wayside.

"But they that receive the spin and the initiatives in stony places, these are they which heareth the bullshit (sorry – do thou forgive me, a false word hath slipped from my lips: I say rather not the bullshit but the modernising) and at once thinketh it cool and verily the latest thing since sliced supernatural sandwiches.

"Yet these have no root, for they have not received the appropriate training, neither the education in the gospel of modernisation; and when the Fogeys and they that are of the Old Farts and such that are backward-looking People do mock them and satirise them and say, as it might be, 'Hast thou heard the latest? It's bloody crackers! And verily thou couldst not make it up,' they are offended and fall away from the coolness of the modernising which they have heard, and loseth their cutting edge.

"They that receive the gospel of modernisation among thorns are they which hearken unto it positively but are tempted away by the fogeyishness and unreconstructed conservatism which speaketh of the good old days and are led away, as it happeneth, unto the *Carlton Club* or the cricket ground which is called *Lord's*. These are they that receive the gospel of modernisation among thorns.

"But they that are effectively trained in all the relevant training courses (of the which there are legion), and that have their consciousness raised by the education which is Politically-Correct, these are they that do reinvent themselves and do stick posters in the windows of their houses as a promo for the Bureaucrat and all his works. This is the seed which falleth on good ground."

And they say unto him, "Now thou speakest plain and thy riddles are no riddles and thy jargon be dejargonified before our eyes and lo, we will serve the modernisation all the days of our life."

"Yeah," saith Andy, "we've really swallowed the bullshit!"

And he addeth, "Just testing – that be all. Just testing!"

And they began to fall all about that place in their laughter.

BOSSY spake unto his groupies another spin also, saying, "A bureaucrat blogged Politically-Correct policies. Of the policies that were Politically-Correct were rich benefits for them that were differently-abled – even for them that were differently-abled but a little; and the tormenting of them that do smoke; and the great modernisation of the laws concerning the bandits and all them that do steal, so that the malefactors, when they are delivered to the judge, be not punished greatly.

"And, behold, while he went on a Freebie in a far country, even he and his wife (which was a woman greatly covetous), they that were rebels of the Bureaucrat's party blogged policies that were politically-incorrect.

"And of the policies that the rebels bloggeth which were politically-incorrect, it happeneth a vow to teach well the infants and the young children; to protect the householders when the thieves break through and steal; and to diminish the tax.

"And when it drew nigh of what is called in their language 'the Election', the minders and the toadies and the physicians of that which is called 'spin' come to the Bureaucrat and do say, 'Leader, didst not thou blog Politically-Correct policies in thy manifesto? From whence then appeareth these that are politically-incorrect?'

"And he saith, 'The bastards have done this!'

"Then were gathered together all the minders, the toadies and the physicians of that which is called 'spin', and they say unto the leader, 'Wilt thou then that we go and tear up the policies that are politically-incorrect and cast them into the fire?'

"And he saith, 'Nay, lest whiles thou burnest the policies that are politically-incorrect, thou burnest the Politically-Correct also. Let them both be blogged together until the Election, that the People might believe that verily the Bureaucrat and his Party do good things. And even the Fogeys and they that are of the Old Farts say, if it were possible: Behold the Bureaucrat – he's a pretty straight kinda guy!

"'Then, when the Election is accomplished, thou canst tear up the politically-incorrect policies and cast them into the fire. For lo, the physicians of that which is called spin in my Party are wiser in their generation than the Opposition.

"'And, behold, I make all things new.'"

And they marvelled that the Latest Thing had given such chicanery unto men.

In those days cometh BOSSY unto his own town, even unto Southend. And he did give presentations in the Health Centre there, insomuch that they were freaked out and said, "Whence hath this man this slickness? Behold, he is smooth, and even very smooth. Is not this the son of Wayne, the hoodie, and Rubella his mother, which is called 'the randy' so that verily she is forever up the duff? And are not these here his brethren, Darren and Trev and Lee and Kevin? And his sisters Megan and Amber, which are called 'slags'?

"Whence then hath this man this pizzazz and this sexiness?"

But the Sarfenders declared, "Where's he get his ego, then?" And they were pissed off with him.

But he saith, "A Guru is a big star except on his own midden and in his own manor."

And BOSSY could do no "spin" there. For they believed not in his street cred.

CHAPTER X

And, behold, they that were of the Old Farts Party drew near and asked him, saying, "Why do thy groupies devour burgers in the streets and dine not in the *Carlton Club*?"

But BOSSY answereth them, "Why art thou and thy groupies so passé, antique and even elitist? Is not the scoff, which is given thee of the Latest Thing, greater than where thou scoffest it? I perceive that in all things thou art uncool."

And they durst not ask him any more questions, save that they condemned him because of the burgers, saying that they were very oafish and oikish.

But he saith unto them, "Not that which goeth into the mouth giveth street cred to a guy, but that which cometh out of the mouth when thou art on the *Stella*.

"And when thou goest forth on the binge, see that thou bingest greatly, so that they that be with thee say, 'Jesus – verily he doth get a lot down his neck!'

"Then that which thou dost get down thy neck shall proceed

outward again even through the mouth and thou shalt throw up exceedingly. Then shall thy gut be ready the second time to receive what thou bingest. And they shall say, 'Verily that lad hath got no clack!'

"Then shalt thou have honour among them that binge with thee and which, as the Fogeys say, do throw up 'all over the sodding street and they ought to be horsewhipped and put in the stocks'."

And BOSSY went from thence into the country around Islington and Camden. And, behold, a woman of Camden cometh out of *Waitrose* and saith unto him, "Have mercy on me thou Son of Dave; my daughter is grievously vexed with the Princess Di Syndrome.

"And, behold, she hath the *bulimia* and dreameth at nights and in the daytime also of that which is called 'landmines' and she goeth after all the men which be rich and totally naff. Moreover she saith 'Yah' all the day long and in the night-season also. And if it so happeneth that any man bring unto her a book, her tongue saith it be a 'buwerck'; and if he ask of her to take a look, she openeth her mouth but a little space and saith 'luwerck'.

"And, behold, she looketh ever to the ground while she raiseth her eyes, so that the Fogeys do look upon her and say, 'What a trollop! See how she simpereth!'

"And – "

But BOSSY saith, "Woman hold thy peace! Verily I am already persuaded that thy daughter hath the legion of devils."

And he saith, "She hath the abundance of nuttiness to make the whole fruitcake – even unto a great fruitcake."

And his groupies say among themselves, "What a frigging tart this one! This'll test his therapeutic skill all right!"

But he, knowing what was in their hearts, saith, "Leave her alone – for her daughter is grievously tormented."

And, behold, her mother saith, "Oh no, you've got it wrong there. It's not *her* that's tormented. She loves all the fuss. It's *me* she drives mad!"

And he saith, "This kind cometh out only with much prayer and fasting."

The woman saith unto him, "She don't do no fasting. She stuffeth herself like there's no tomorrow, like, then throws it all up – just like Di used to do, in fact. And she don't pray – not as such. She's got these New Age Counsellors, see!"

When BOSSY heard these words he was wroth and saith unto the woman concerning the New Age Counsellors, "Not everyone that calleth himself or herself 'New Age Counsellor' is a New Age Counsellor. Behold, he or she hath need to submit himself or herself to that which is called 'the three-week professional training course'. Then shall he or she put up the plate on his or her door and be called 'New Age Counsellor'; and receive unto himself or herself the riches thereof."

And the woman entreateth him with great sorrow, "Sir, come and take a butcher's at my daughter."

But he answered and said, "Call no man 'Sir'. For that be elitist. Neither speak thou any more of 'butchers'. For it is written, 'Thou shalt go veggie and even vegan.'"

And he saith, "Moreover, thou dwellest in Camden and I am sent but to the lost sheep of the house of Southend."

But she was exceeding wroth and rent her garments and with a loud voice saith unto him, "There aren't many sodding sheep in Southend, mate!"

And all the groupies did fall about.

Then BOSSY chucketh the woman under the chin and saith, "Thou hast answered to all things well. I have not seen such *chutzpah* – no, not even on my package holiday in Eilat. Go thy way. Thy feistiness sufficeth."

And her daughter was made clean of the Princess Di Syndrome in that self-same hour.

When BOSSY came into the coasts of Ramsgate and Margate, he saith, "On Margate sands I can connect nothing with nothing."

And the groupies say unto one another, "What is this 'Margate sands' of which he speaketh? And that he can connect 'nothing with nothing'? Behold, we cannot tell what he saith."

But he answered, "How is it that ye know not of that I do speak? Behold, I say unto you, these sands which thou callest 'Margate' shall lie desolate and the whole land shall be waste."

And no man durst ask him any more questions. But Matt saith, "It appeareth the Moderniser General is tormented by the devil of elitism. Send ye therefore for the wireless and play unto him that which is called *Poetry Please*. Verily that knocketh out of him the elitism."

And when they came unto Margate, by the very whelk stall and the amusements that be in the arcade there, BOSSY saith unto them, "Whom do the punters say that I, the Son of Wayne, am?"

And they say, "Some say that thou art Jak the Aquatherapist come back from the dead; some the prophet Karl Marx, or Stalin which was called Joe."

He saith unto them, "But who say ye that I am?"

And Simmy answered and said, "Thou art the Facilitator, the Moderniser General, the Boy with the Latest Thing."

And BOSSY answered and said unto him, "Smart of thee, Simmy. For neither the horoscope in *The Star* hath revealed this unto thee, nor the *Old Moore's Almanack*; but the Latest Thing in Cloud Cuckoo Land.

"And I say also unto thee that thou art Pete and upon this rock star I will build my Project; and the forces of conservatism shall not prevail against it, neither the Fogeys nor they that are yesterday's news. And I will give thee the PIN number of Cloud Cuckoo Land: and whatsoever thou shalt modernise in Southend shall be modernised in Cloud Cuckoo Land; and whatsoever thou shalt ban in all the Nanny State shall be banned in Cloud Cuckoo Land until the Great Modernisation be complete."

Then charged he his groupies that they should tell no one that he was the Guy with the Latest Thing.

From that time forth BOSSY began to show his groupies how

that he must go to the Great City and suffer lousy notices and score zilch in the opinion polls, and have the piss taken out of him by the Fogeys and be patronised. Even that he would be satirised. But that after three days he would be known as the Comeback Kid.

Then Pete took him and began to chew him out, saying, "Be it far from thee, Moderniser General, to be satirised and patronised and have the piss taken out of thee. These things shall not be done unto thee – not while I'm in charge of the promos!"

But BOSSY turned and said unto him, "Get thee behind me, Chief Fogey! – for thou art an offence to me. For thou savourest not which parts of the Project are the Latest Thing, but which are, like, yucky and unreconstructed!"

And he saith, "If any guy backs my Project and, like, is on my bandwagon, let him get wasted for my sake. And let him be patron-ised and satirised and have the piss taken. For whosoever will lose his street cred for my sake and the sake of the Project shall find it.

"For what is a guy profited if he shall get all the promos and the fab notices but lose his image? Or what shall a guy give in exchange for his iconic status?

"And the Guy with the Latest Thing shall come in the Glitz of the Latest Thing with his Vibes and his Archvibes; and all his groupies and cronies shall receive their payoff.

"But verily I say unto you, there be guys standing here which shall not have the piss taken or even be satirised until they have seen the Guy with the Latest Thing accomplish the Great Modernisation."

CHAPTER XI

Then cometh BOSSY unto the City and behold, a junior partner in one of the law firms there, tempting him, saith, "Moderniser, what shall I do to be totally Politically-Correct?"

And he saith, "What is written in the Project? How readest thou?"

And he, answering, saith, "Thou shalt love the Latest Thing even to die for. And fawn over complete strangers and People you've never bloody-well heard of with all thy mawkishness."

And he said unto him, "Thou hast answered like unto the perfect new man and with ace street cred. This do and thou shalt be altogether Politically-Correct."

But he, pedantic, stiff-necked and hard of heart (as it be with the lawyers) saith, "And who is the complete stranger and person I've never bloody-well heard of?"

And BOSSY, answering, saith, "This guy went down from Chelsea to Dagenham and, as he passed through the East End, fell among hoodies and muggers which stripped him of his designer clobber and pissed off leaving him, like, duffed up.

"And, by chance, there came down a certain man which profiteth by the tobacco industry that way, and when he saw the guy he passed by on the other side.

"And likewise a four-by-four owner who, it happened, was also an international arms dealer, when he was at the place, came and looked on him and passed by on the other side.

"But a certain social worker which worketh for the equal opportunities among the disadvantaged and them that are Gay and vulnerable in the deprived inner city, when she journeyed came where he was and went to him. And she was a lesbian.

"And she sticketh on a sticking plaster and giveth him the Echinacea and, behold, she saith, 'Verily the person that hath done this is a victim which needeth professional help!'

"And she shoved him in the back of the *Volvo* and taketh him to the hostel for them that be the underprivileged – which were aforetime the dossers, the shiftless wonders and the layabouts – and handeth a pile of tokens and vouchers to the do-gooder which doeth good there and saith, 'See that thou compliest with all that be in accordance with health and safety and do thou take care for, for any forms which thou fillest not in threefold thou shalt receive bollockings double for all thy non-compliance.'

"Which now of these three thinkest thou was mawkish to the one that fell among thieves and was exceeding sentimental over him?"

And the lawyer saith, "The lesbian social worker – even she that doeth Political-Correctness unto him that fell among hoodies."

And he saith, "Go and do thou likewise."

But the lawyer saith, "Look, mate, I just wanna be Politically-Correct. I'm not gonna be no brown-hatter for thee or anyone else!"

And after six days BOSSY taketh Pete, Jim and Jon and bringeth them to the press conference. And, behold, he really sparkled and dazzled and his face shone in *The Sun* when they did the photo-shoot; and his gear was white as anything worn by that man which is called Martin Bell.

And, behold, there appeared unto them the President of the EU and the Secretary-General of the UN.

And the groupies were freaked out. Then Pete saith unto him, "This is what it's all about, eh? Let's take over three studios – one for thee, one for the President and the other for the Secretary-General. We could run the world from here!"

While he yet spake, the strobe lights flashed and the captions rolled and the link man went into the big promo, "And now let's hear it for the Moderniser General!"

And lo, they all kitteneth.

But he saith, "Have ye no kittens. I'm just practising!"

At the same time, came the groupies unto BOSSY and asked him, "Who shall be most famous when the Final Dianafication shall come?"

And BOSSY calleth a TV presenter with a voice like unto a little child and set him in the midst of them and saith, "Except ye become babyish and, like, totally infantilised, ye cannot enter on the Dianafication.

"Whosoever shall gurgle and coo and affect utter childishness and gather unto themselves soft toys – as it happeneth the teddy bear or some of those *Smurfs* that be handed out on *Children in Need* – the same shall be greatest in the Dianafication.

"But whoso shall offend one of these totally infantilised airheads and commandeth her or him, 'Grow up!' it were better for them that balloons were hanged about their necks and they were sent to the naughty corner."

And Pete cometh to him and saith, "Facilitator, we know that thou art clued up more than anybody when it cometh to the Standard Practice, and that, behold, of all them that be Politically-Correct and completely modernised, there is none more Politically-Correct nor modernised than thee. Tell us, how oft shall my neighbour offend me and I sue him? Till seven times?"

And he saith, "I say not unto thee seven times, but seventy times seven. For is it not written in the Standard Practice, 'Thou shalt shop thy neighbour as thyself'?

"For verily, if thou findest that thou thyself offend against what is in the Standard Practice and shalt see thyself on *Crimewatch,* thou shalt surrender thyself to the Politically-Correct Police."

Then come the Fogeys unto him with them that were of the Old Farts, and they say, tempting him, "Facilitator, is it lawful for a man to put away his wife for every cause?"

And he saith, "Have ye not read how the Latest Thing hath made an offence discrimination on grounds of gender? How say ye then of these things which be no more, for verily they are all modernised, these things 'man' and 'woman' of which ye speak?

"For according to the Latest Thing, a man or a woman shall leave his or her mother and father – or as it happeneth her or his one-parent family (for that her or his dad hath done a runner or her or his old lady getteth pissed off and shacketh up with her lesby girlfriend) and move in with any tosser he or she lusteth after. And this thing shall be called 'a relationship'.

"But and if she or he waxeth bored of her or his new partner, then she or he shall split and go forth seeking someone else to shag. For the children of Modern Britain are not given in marriage, save if it happeneth they be puftas or they that are of the brown-hatting community which constantly beseech the Bureaucrat that they might marry.

"What therefore the Latest Thing hath joined together, let any woman or man put asunder."

And one cometh to him and saith, "Fab Moderniser General, what shall I do that I may be cool and Politically-Correct?"

And he saith, "Why callest thou me 'Fab'? There is none fab but the Latest Thing. But if thou wouldst be cool and enter into that life which is Politically-Correct, thou shalt keep the statutes and ordinances which are in the Standard Practice."

And he answereth, "Which?"

BOSSY saith, "Thou shalt not be racist, neither shalt thou be sexist and thou shalt seek equal opportunities on a non-discriminatory basis all the days of thy life."

The young man saith unto him, "All these statutes and ordinances have I kept since the first day of my modernisation when I did enter the re-education course decreed by the Nanny State. What further evidence of compliance need I?"

And BOSSY said, "One thing thou lackest: give greatly of thy substance unto *Red Nose Day* or, as it happeneth, *Children in Need* and thou shalt have kudos amongst them that are modernised."

But when the young man heard this saying, he went away sorrowing – for he loveth not in his heart the mawkishness of *Red Nose Day*, neither the humourless abasements which are that which is called *Children in Need*.

CHAPTER XII

And BOSSY goeth the third time to the region round about the Serpentine and, behold, his groupies were with him. And when he was set, he began to teach them concerning role models, saying, "A certain man which dwelleth in Hampstead had two sons. And the younger of them said unto his father, 'Give me the portion of goods that falleth to me that I may go unto Brighton and get totally wrecked and shag everything that moveth.'

"And his father saith, 'Be it unto thee even as thou desirest.'

"And not many days hence the younger son gathered all together and took his journey into Brighton wherein he did get totally wrecked and lo, he shaggeth everything that moveth, whether man or woman or beast or creeping thing that creepeth over the face of the earth, on a completely non-discriminatory basis.

"And when he had spent all, there was a downturn in the bond market and he was cleaned out. And, behold, he went and dossed with them that do doss, even with the druggies, the alcys and them that were two sandwiches short of a miraculous picnic, being, like, totally out of it on the meths and that which is called 'glue'.

"And he would fain have filled his belly with the remnants of the junk food cartons which the yobbos do cast down all over the frigging place. And none in that town would render unto him even so much as the cellophane off his *ciabatta,* neither the aroma of her *cappuccino.*

"And when he came to himself he saith, 'How many *au pairs* and cleaning ladies in my father's house in Hampstead have *ciabatta* and *guacamole* enough and to spare, and I fall faint with the druggies, the alcys and them that be two sandwiches short of the miraculous picnic?'

"'Behold, I am purposed what I will do. I will arise and go to the old feller and say unto him: Dad, I've screwed up big time and am no more worthy to be called thy son. Make me as one of thy cleaning ladies or even like unto one of the *au pairs* in thine household which peradventure my elder brother yet screweth.'

"And he arose and hitcheth along the A23 until he cometh to the South Circular Road, whence he taketh shanks's pony even unto Hampstead.

"But when he was yet a great way off, behold, his elder brother seeth him and saith unto his father, 'Behold, that sodding waster's back – him that did bugger off unto Brighton and getteth totally wrecked these many months, and shaggeth everything that moveth non-discriminatingly as to whether it be man or woman or beast or creeping thing that creepeth over the face of the whole earth.'

"But his father saith, 'Bring forth the designer clobber and put it on him and bring hither the fatted calf and kill it. And let there be a disco and other such noisome filth. For this my son hath gone forth and asserted his own identity and distanced himself from the narrow confines of the family unit, and he now returneth a mature human person with his own self-esteem.'

"But the hired caterers say unto him, 'Lo, there is no fatted calf for (thou must remember, thou silly sod) we all went veggie according as the Latest Thing hath commanded us. Besides, the EU directeth long ago that slaughter of animals wast prohibited under section 36 of the European Food, Health and Safety Regulations.'

"And his father saith, 'Ye have spoken rightly. What the hell was I thinking about!'

"And he commandeth that they bring forth the nut roast and the rocket salad.

"Now his elder brother was on the patio and, as he drew nigh unto the house, he heard the noise of the disco. And he calleth one of the *au pairs* and enquired as to what manner of salutation this might be. And she saith unto him, 'C'est le pillock thy kid frère qui est rétrouvé, comme, après he screweth around, comme, touts les mois sans-discrimination, homme, femme, bête ou les escargots à Brighton et touts-les-points sud.'

"And he was wroth and would not enter into the disco. Therefore came out unto him his father and saith, 'Sulk thou not, thou anal-retentive prat! For thou hast never gone out so much as one night on the piss, nor discoverest thou for thyself thy identity or thy role; neither hast thou any self-esteem. Rejoice with me, for thy brother wast screwed up even as thou art. But behold, he findeth his image and hath become an icon and a role model and verily he is filled with self-esteem.'"

Then cometh BOSSY into the City and seeth all the brokers and traders which return from their third charlie break that morning and do take care over their sojourn and ease in faraway countries with their concubines and partners.

And he saith, "Behold, how hardly shall a capitalist or he that worshippeth the globalised economy enter into Cloud Cuckoo Land! It is easier for a pantomime horse to go limbo dancing beneath the loo door than for a capitalist to enter into Cloud Cuckoo Land."

And his groupies say unto him, "Who, then, can achieve personal fulfilment?"

He saith, "With persons this is impossible, but with the Latest Thing all things are possible."

Then Pete saith, "Lo, we have given up all to follow the Latest Thing, what shall be in it for us, therefore?"

He saith, "Verily I say unto thee, that ye which have followed the Latest Thing on Earth shall, when the Great Modernisation be accomplished and Political-Correctness shall rule throughout the land, sit in the Court of the European Superstate and shall be called 'bossy' even as I am BOSSY."

And it came to pass the day after that he went into a town named Cheam and many of his groupies went with him and much People. And when he came nigh unto *The Cemetery Tavern* a paralytic man was carried out, the only son of his single mother, for behold, his father hath done a runner before he was born and the Child Support Agency findeth him not.

And when BOSSY saw the single mother he was minded to interfere whether she liketh it or no.

And he came and touched the beery one. And they that were his brethren and acquaintance stood still.

And he saith unto him that wast paralytic, "Arise!"

And he that was, like, totally out of it, stood up and saith, "Pint o' *Stella*!"

Then delivered he him to his single mother and she saith,

"O God – and I thought I was going to get some peace and quiet from that one this afternoon!"

And they all freaked out and said, "He hath done all things well. He maketh both the Old Farts to get the hump and the totally arseholed to get more down their necks!"

And they departed into *The Cemetery Tavern* for the hour that is called "Blessed Hour".

And one of the Old Farts desireth him that he would dine with him in the *Carlton Club*. And he went into the *Carlton Club* and did sit down at meat with him – for the fish it wast "off".

And, behold, one of the women who ran the Alternative Therapy and Holistic Counselling shop, when she knew that BOSSY wast eating fish with the Fogeys, brought an alabaster box with her aromatherapy. And, her eyes watering for the niff of the garlic that was there, began to administer to him the specimen trial course of her aromatherapy.

She taketh also his feet and practiseth her reflexology there.

And the Fogey which had bidden him to the *Carlton Club* – Simmy (not Pete) – began to say, "Send her away! For this is that which is called Mad Magda and, behold, she hath the iniquities of the New Age like unto the very devil!"

But BOSSY, answering, said unto him, "Simmy, I have somewhat to say unto thee!"

And he, willing to justify himself, saith, "Facilitator, say on."

And BOSSY opened his mouth and saith, "There was a barfly in the *Carlton Club* which paid the bar bills of two Old Farts: the one of three score Euros and the other an hundred. And he frankly forgave them both.

"Tell me, therefore, which of these two Old Farts will love him the most?"

And Simmy saith unto him, "The one to whom he forgave most."

And BOSSY said, "Thou hast judged rightly." And he turneth to Mad Magda and saith unto Simmy, "Seest thou this woman?

I entered into thy Fogeys' Club, body lotion for my body didst thou not give me, nor designer uppers for my bipolar disorder; but she hath never ceased to render unto me her aromatherapy and to minister unto my feet, and hence my whole being holistically, with her reflexology.

"Wherefore I say unto thee, her alternative therapy and even her new-ageiness hath made her a qualified practitioner. And her former loopiness (which was in any the wise but a little loopiness) is no loopiness unto me."

And he turneth to Mad Magda and saith, "Thy caring in the community hath made thee socially-included, and thy touchy-feeliness qualifieth thee for the Princess Di Medal for Sentimentality."

But the Fogeys that sat at meat with him (for as it was written aforetime, the fish wast "off") wondered within themselves and said, "Who is this that excuseth the loopiness and doth make even them that are off their very trolleys to be socially-included?"

And, behold, he departed out of the *Carlton Club* and the household that was filled with Old Farts, and cometh into his own city.

CHAPTER XIII

And when he was come into the country round about the Isle of Sheppey, the multitudes pressed upon him for to hear his presentation and his counselling and to marvel at his wondrous narrative and spin. And they said within themselves, "Behold, he spins with authority, not as the Fogeys."

The whole throng came upon him and he lift up his eyes and saith to Phil, "Whence shall we buy *ciabatta*, *formaggio* and *guacamole* that these may eat?"

(And this he said to prove him, for he himself knew what he would do.)

And Phil said, "Verily there be not sufficient Eyetie nosh – no, not in all Islington – to feed this lot."

One of the groupies, Andy, Sim's brother (which was called Pete), saith unto him, "There's a lad here which hath a small basket of garlic bread – like unto that which is on the starter menu in *Carluccio's* – and two sardines; but what are they among so many?"

And he saith, "Be the sardines in olive oil or brine?"

He answereth and saith, "Nay, Administrator, but they be in tomato sauce."

He saith, "Wondrous – for verily the tomato sauce is my fave!"

And BOSSY said, "Make the multitude to sit down."

Now there was much grass in the place, so they sat down, in number about five thousand, and smoked it.

And Matty the VAT man saith, "Not a bad turnout, Guv – but not as many as came to the *Rolling Stones*. And, behold, the *Stones* fans were not anhungered for they were all on that which is called 'charlie' and even on the 'E' which do turn off the anhungeredness, man."

And BOSSY took the small basket of garlic bread and the fave sardines in the tomato sauce and, when he had raised his eyes and uttered something mawkish and fanciful concerning Fair Trade and Debt Relief, distributed the small basket of garlic bread and the two sardines to the groupies, and the groupies to them that were set down.

And they all did eat and were filled.

And lo, his groupies say amongst themselves, "How'd he do that, then?"

And BOSSY did hear the words which the groupies spake concerning the apparently miraculous nosh, and he saith, "Although it wasn't a miracle in the way that old-fashioned, primitive and out-of-date religious cranks use the word 'miracle', it was an even greater miracle in a way. For if People in the rich countries of the West will support political parties that have a global policy of foreign aid, then the underprivileged People in Africa and many other such places will be fed and live happy lives under the dictatorships which this Western money subsidiseth."

And when they heard these words, they were all amazed, and Andy turneth to Pete and saith, "If thou wilt believe that, then thou wilt believe anything!"

But Pete answereth, "I didn't understand a frigging word of it. English as a foreign language, if you ask me."

But BOSSY turneth unto him and rebuketh him, saying, "Verily it be not the English as a foreign language, but the language of Cloud Cuckoo Land."

Jim saith, "Shall we gather up the fragments, that nothing be lost?"

But Jon saith, "Nay – but leave the place like unto an shit-heap as the custom be after these gigs. Hast thou not read what the Guru saith:

'The days shall come when many shall utter compassion for that which is called the environment;

'Nevertheless, they shall leave every place wherein they enter like unto an shit-heap;

'And some other mugs will have to clear it up.'"

And BOSSY saith unto Jon, "Thou hast well spoken."

Then the multitudes, when they had seen the modern "miracle" of Debt Relief and foreign aid – not the primitive religious twaddle which wast aforetime – said, "Verily this is that Moderniser that should come into the world!"

And when they were come away from that region, they came again unto Islington. And, behold, there came a man named Percy, and he was in the senior management team at the BBC, which besought BOSSY that he would come unto his apartment, for he saith, "My daughter hath the Attention Deficit Hyperactivity Disorder (ADHD). This group of disorders is characterised by: early onset; a combination of overactive, poorly modulated behaviour with marked inattention and lack of persistent task involvement; and pervasiveness over situations and persistence over time of these behavioural characteristics.

"It is widely thought that constitutional abnormalities play a crucial role in the genesis of these disorders, but knowledge on specific aetiology is lacking at present. In recent years the use of the diagnostic term 'Attention Deficit Disorder' for these syndromes has been promoted, though it implies a knowledge of psychological processes that is not yet available, and it suggests the inclusion of anxious, preoccupied, or 'dreamy' apathetic subjects whose problems display alternative aetiologies. However, it is clear that, from the point of view of behaviour, problems of inattention constitute a central feature of these hyperkinetic syndromes.

"Hyperkinetic syndromes always arise early in development (usually in the first five years of life). Their chief characteristics are lack of persistence in activities that require cognitive involvement, and a tendency to move from one activity to another without completing any one, together with disorganised, ill-regulated, and excessive activity.

"Several other abnormalities may be associated with these disorders. Hyperkinetic subjects are often reckless and impulsive, prone to accidents, and find themselves in disciplinary trouble because of unthinking (rather than deliberately defiant) breaches of rules. Their relationships with adults are often socially disinhibited, with a lack of normal caution and reserve. They are unpopular with their peers and may become isolated. Cognitive impairment is common, and specific delays in motor and language development are disproportionately frequent.

"Secondary complications include dissocial behaviour and low self-esteem. There is, accordingly, considerable overlap between hyperkinesis and other patterns of disruptive behaviour, such as 'Unsocialised Conduct Disorder' (UCD) and 'Perverse Ratiocination and Trouble-causing' (PRAT)."

BOSSY slept.

But he that was a member of the senior management team besought him in a loud voice, saying, "Moreover the Fogeys and they that are of the Old Farts Party do say that she hath not the

Attention Deficit Hyperactivity Disorder Syndrome, for that be a vain thing fondly invented and that verily there be no Attention Deficit Hyperactivity Disorder Syndrome. And besides all these things, today is *Attention Deficit Hyperactivity Disorder Syndrome Day*."

And BOSSY had mercy on Percy and said, "What then do the Fogeys and they that are of the Old Farts Party say concerning thy daughter?"

He answereth, "That she is a naughty little cunt and needeth the bloody good hiding."

Now, for that it was *Attention Deficit Hyperactivity Disorder Syndrome Day*, there was much People in the place and they watched him to see what he would do. For she that hath the PRAT disease entered where they were sitting and cast herself down before them and made a great tumult so that the People were sore afraid.

And BOSSY looketh upon her and saith, "Behold, she needeth not the bloody good hiding as the Fogeys do vainly believe, but the Cognitive Therapy and that which is called 'Positive Reinforcement'."

And she that hath the PRAT crieth out, "Piss off, wilt thou! They've tried all that psychology crap and I'll still do as I sodding well like. Gimme another Big Mac!"

Then her father, sorrowing, saith unto the PRAT, "Verily thou hast consumed this day even unto six of that which is called 'Big Mac'. Thinkest thou not, darling, that thou hast consumed sufficient unto the day?"

But she crieth out the more and saith, "Just piss off – and make this BOSSY boots piss off with thee!"

And BOSSY arose and took her by the hand and saith, "We'd better give her some *methylphenidate* or *dexamfetamine*, then – or it happeneth thou hast some *atomoxetine* in thy bathroom cabinet?"

But the PRAT did spit and saith unto him, "Get thy hands off me, thou dirty old sod! What – art thou a sodding paedophile, then?"

And Percy saith, "It doth not avail to give unto her the medicines, for verily she doth throw them up. For she hath the *bulimia* also, the which she suffereth since *Princess Diana Day.*" And he began to be exceeding sorrowful.

Then BOSSY arose and left that place for, behold, he could do no miracle there. And the People wondered.

CHAPTER XIV

And he cometh again into Southend and unto the offices of the Services which are called "Social" therein. And, behold, many of them that laboured in the Services which are called "Social" were compelled to be delivered of the Officer unto the Magistrate and from the Magistrate unto the Judge and from the Judge thence unto the whole Committee of Enquiry, for that they had suffered the little children to be offended and scourged by their parents; and they had not removed them from the households of their parents which did scourge and offend them, even grievously.

And BOSSY saith unto the Officer, "Wherefore compellest thou these our Social Workers to be delivered unto the Magistrate and from the Magistrate unto the Judge and from the Judge thence unto the whole Committee of Enquiry? What evil have they done?"

The Officer saith unto him, "For that they did not remove the little ones which are scourged and offended out of the hands of their parents which do scourge and offend them, and from their households."

But he was wroth and layeth hands suddenly on the Officer and saith, "Hast thou not heard how it is written by the Bureaucrat, and in all the scrolls of that which is the Standard Practice, that verily they that are the Social Workers err not, neither is any fault to be found in them whatsoever?"

And lo, the Officer was much discomfited and he saith, "But Facilitator, the little ones are grievously tormented and the marks of their torment appear in their flesh so that they sit not down, nor even lie on their beds, for the sore agony that doth torment them.

"And it happeneth not but that their parents did this thing – for there was none other to do like unto it. And besides all these things, there passeth the whole year in the which the Social Workers did write down all that came to pass concerning the little ones in their Case Histories.

"Yet do they not deliver them from the hands of their parents which did this evil. For this cause are they delivered unto the Magistrate and from the Magistrate unto the Judge and from the Judge thence unto the whole Committee of Enquiry."

But BOSSY lift up his eyes and gazed steadfastly into Cloud Cuckoo Land and commanded that the Social Workers be set free, saying, "Whoso hateth his or her parents, it shall be forgiven him or her. And he or she that scourge and offend these little ones like-wise. But whoso speaketh ill against any of these our Social Workers, it were better for him or her that he or she were socially-excluded and cast into the depths of the Council Black List from whence neither she nor he nor any of their dependent relatives be any more considered for re-housing on a nicer part of the sink estate."

And so, after that he had decreed a record of these events be indented into their very Career Dossiers and commanded that from henceforth they be monitored, the Magistrate let them go their way.

And straightway they did return unto the Officer that had (as they say in their language) "shopped" them and did make at that place a solemn vow: "We'll get the bastard. Nobody pisses about with us!"

And BOSSY returned unto his own city and his groupies were with him.

And he began to say unto them in his doctrine, "It was said aforetime that ye are the salt of the earth. But I say unto you, take thee no more salt, for it raiseth thy blood pressure and it may be that ye crumple with an heart attack or, as it might be, a stroke."

And they marvelled that the Latest Thing had given such wisdom unto men.

Then drew near all the Fogeys and the Old Farts for to hear him. And the Fogeys murmured and said among themselves, "This man receiveth oiks and yobbos and them that are called 'vulnerable' and 'disadvantaged persons from the inner city' and 'differently-abled' People and them that do have 'alternative lifestyles'; also the 'multicultural' –"

But his groupies rebuked them, saying, "OK. OK. We haven't time for the whole list!"

And BOSSY, turning to the Fogeys and Old Farts, saith unto them, "Which of you having an hundred sheep, if he or she loseth one of them on the Sabbath day, doth not leave the ninety-and-nine, go to the pub and catch the *Eurostar* first thing Monday morning to put in his or her missing livestock claim under the terms of the Common Agricultural Policy?

"And when he or she receiveth the compensation to which he or she is entitled, he or she putteth the cash in his or her pocket and rejoiceth. And when he or she cometh home, he or she saith unto his or her colleagues, 'Let's go get pissed. It's my round. For, behold, I do screw the taxpayer this umpteenth time!'

"And lo, Cloud Cuckoo Land is within thee."

And none durst answer him a word.

And he saith, "Behold, it is not the Politically-Correct which require re-education and consciousness-raising so that they be aware of the special needs of minorities, but the unreconstructed reactionaries and Old Farts, like unto you."

Then one of them, which was an Old Fart, saith, "Facilitator, we know that thou hast been on all the appropriate training courses and that thou hast skills more than any man can number. Tell us, therefore, what will become of transgressors at the last?

"For Moses gave us a Law and the prophets, and by this Law they that do sin shall perish and they that are righteous shall receive everlasting life. And Jesus hath said that the righteous shall have everlasting inheritance but the sinners shall depart unto everlasting fire. Tell us, therefore, what dost thou say?"

And BOSSY looked on them, sorrowing, and saith, "O fools and slow of heart to believe all that the prophets did tell thee! For Moses indeed gaveth the Law, and Jesus hath said that they which are sinners shall depart into everlasting fire.

"But I say unto you, ye shall not be judgmental in anything. For Moses and the prophets and Jesus spake unto the People as the People understanded in the old time. But in the Great Modernisation, behold, the former things are done away. And lo, in modern times there is no sin, neither is there guiltiness – for guiltiness doth take away thy self-esteem; and it is a grievous thing to lose one's self-esteem.

"There be, therefore, no sin nor wrongdoing. For hearken thou unto my saying that in these times which are called 'progressive' and 'emancipated', there is only that which is called 'lifestyle'. And everyone can do as he or she sodding well likes – except that which be politically-incorrect.

"For all manner of what was formerly sin, and all manner of iniquity, shall be forgiven thee – except the sin of political-incorrectness for the which there is no forgiveness."

When he heard this saying, the Old Fart departed sorrowing – for he was very politically-incorrect.

And BOSSY saith unto his groupies, "Behold, there was a certain fat cat which was clothed in *Armani* and fine *Calvin Kleins* and which did nosh sumptuously every day at *Café de la Comment est Votre Père?*

"And there was a certain underprivileged person named Laz, which was in receipt of benefits, laid at his gate full of psychosomatic skin disorders, and desiring to be filled with the leftovers from the promos that the fat cat splasheth out on for the hangers-on in his media empire.

"Moreover the *paparazzi* came and did photograph him for the photo-shoot which appeareth on the TV news for the fulfilment of the mawkishness of the People which do love to behold that which doth resemble picturesque poverty.

"And it came to pass that Laz's benefits were greatly increased and, behold, he findeth it among his substance to install the digital telly, the cool new *PlayStation* for his sprogs and the chav jewellery for his slag.

"But the fat cat was indicted under section two, subsection 39 of the Companies Act and cast into prison.

"And in prison he lift up his eyes and said, 'O thou Minister for Equal Opportunities, have mercy on me and send Laz that he may photocopy his latest fraudulent appeal to the Benefits Office, that I might send it under mine own name and partake of the handouts thereof.'

"But the Minister for Equal Opportunities saith, 'Son, remember that thou in thy fatcatness received thy megalifestyle, and likewise Laz only the state benefits whereby he benefiteth – and whatsoever other he did accordingly scam. Now he hath his benefits increased and thou hast been nobbled.

"'And beside all this, between Laz and thyself social discrimination on the basis of class and economic determinism is fixed, so that they which would pass from the scroungers to the superannuated arseholes cannot pass; neither they which are among the bloated plutocrats may pass to the bloody oiks.'

"Then he said, 'I pray thee, Minister for Equal Opportunities, that thou wouldst send Laz to my ex's house, for we have the five sprogs which are also into the wheeler-dealing (and verily thou knowest how it is when thou seekest to make a bob or two on the side – know what I mean?), and tip them off also as to when they are nigh unto being fingered.'

"But the Minister for Equal Opportunities saith, 'They know the usual crooks within the Financial Services Sector – let them hear them.'

"But he saith, 'Nay Mr Minister, but if one of the insider dealers went unto them, they would watch their backs.'

"But the Minister answered and said, 'Behold, if they hear not the usual crooks within the Financial Services Sector, neither will they be persuaded though one should go unto them from the insider dealers.'"

CHAPTER XV

And BOSSY spake a spin unto them to this end, that People ought always to demand their rights and complain, and never get sick of complaining.

"There was in a city a certain Council Official which was no fan of the Latest Thing and pretty much a bastard to boot.

"And there was an old biddy in that city, and she came to him, saying, 'Avenge me of mine adversary. It's those pillocks at number 84. She has men up and down her stairs till all hours and he's never anywhere to be seen. It happeneth he hath done a runner – and frankly, one look at her and I don't blame him. (But that's beside the point.) The little sods ride their motorbikes on the pavement; and their cats do shit on my strawberries.'

"And the Council Official, for that he was a Council Official, doeth nothing about it. But the old biddy was diligent in her complaining and in the demand for her rights withal. And, behold, she writeth letters in the green ink whereof the Official comprehendeth not, for the old biddy had aforetime been at the Comprehensive and therefore she knew not her letters nor even how to write them.

"Moreover, she cometh and standeth beneath the window of the Council Office and maketh a great disturbance, so that the whole Council and they that sat about idle by day and by night in the offices cried out and said unto the Official, 'Can't you get rid of this toe rag which is pestilential by day and by night with her "frigging this" and her "frigging that"?'

"And he would not for a while. But afterward he said within himself, 'Though I have no love for the oiks and the yobbos, and though I dwell in a great house in a nice part of town and not on that Council shit-heap, I am become wearied of her complaining and her jealousy for her rights.

"'I am purposed therefore to avenge her. Not for that her strawberries, behold, they are covered in cat shit, nor for that her neighbour runneth a knocking shop right next door, nor yet for that her sprogs (which verily be pillocks) do ride their motorbikes on the pavement; but for that she hath complied with full compliance with all the statutes and ordinances that must be complied with under the rules governing Compliance and that she hath fulfilled the requirements of that which is called Health and Safety and the responsibilities of council tenants under the Council Tenants' Act, being the Act for the pursuance of all matters which have aught to do with tenants and the aforementioned Council.

"'And besides, she pisseth me off with her freaking whingeing. For a contentious woman and a ceaseless dropping on a very rainy day, are not they like unto each other?'"

When BOSSY had left off his speaking, his groupies say unto him, "Facilitator, we know that thou art a compliant person and Politically-Correct in all that thou dost teach, tell us the meaning of this spin, for we cannot tell what it doth mean."

And he saith, "God – you are thick! It just means that if you shower a guy with enough paperwork and bore his arse off with complaining, you'll get what you want in the end!"

But they comprehended not this saying and, behold, it was hid from their eyes.

And he spake this spin unto certain that trusted in themselves that they were totally compliant and despised others: "Behold, a Politically-Correct person and a Fogey went on a chat show on *Crap TV*. And the Fogey saith, 'I'm not PC at all. I think it's totalitarianism-lite. It's a way of stifling free speech. It's a denial of English political history and the historic settlements which always guaranteed healthy discussion and disagreement.'

"And the studio audience laughed him to scorn.

"But the Politically-Correct person, when the fawning Quiz Master bade her come unto the microphone, saith, 'Behold, I contribute to every tsunami relief going and ever on *Princess Di Day* do I throw my teddy bears and weep these many buckets. I patronise everybody on the scale of equality, regardless of race, gender or religious orientation. And lo, when it cometh to the *Red Nose Day*, I do put on my red nose which is exceeding red.'

"I say unto you that this PC person is of a truth more cool and loveth the Latest Thing more than the Fogey which shall be cast into outer darkness and not allowed to come on the telly a second time."

And when they heard these things, behold, they marvelled that the Latest Thing had given such expertise unto persons.

And as BOSSY passed by, he saw a man that was partially-sighted from his birth. And his groupies said unto him, "Facilitator, who was politically-incorrect, this man or his parents that he was born partially-sighted? For happeneth it not that sexism and racism are handed down through the genes even unto the third and fourth generations of them that be politically-incorrect?"

BOSSY saith, "Both this man and his parents were politically-incorrect – and this bugger still is!"

And, behold, he that was partially-sighted began to cry out in a loud voice so many words which were politically-incorrect that no man could number them. For it happeneth that a differently-abled person came that way, and, behold, the politically-incorrect man crieth, "I can see you – you cripple!"

And whosoever passed by that way, he did cry after in his political-incorrectness: "Fatso!" and "God she's ugly – what a sight!" and even "Coon!" Moreover, the politically-incorrect man wore a coat of fur and smoketh the *Gauloises.*

When he saw BOSSY he cried out the more, "Ah, so it's you, Facilitator, Moderniser General! What have I to do with thee? Hast thou come to torment me?"

But BOSSY, when he drew near, had pity on him and bade him be silent. And he was silent, and the People watched him to see what he would do. And BOSSY took from his scrip a pair of the coolest contact lenses from *Specsavers*, laid them on him that was politically-incorrect and partially-sighted.

And he saith, "Take thou these *Euphemismia* lenses and be thou healed of thy partially-sightedness, and it happeneth also that, seeing, thou mayest be delivered of thy political-incorrectness."

And straightway he that was partially-sighted saw clearly and he saith no more "Fatso!" but "Ooh, look – there's a beautiful and generously proportioned person!" and "What a nice young man from an ethnic minority!"

And the People marvelled that such miracles were done among them. But the Fogeys and the Old Farts did murmur within themselves and one saith, "This be not he that was politically-incorrect – for no man maketh the politically-incorrect to be Politically-Correct."

And BOSSY, when he heard these things, was wroth and saith, "This sign is for the hardness of your heart, for verily it is a sign of the Latest Thing."

And for their hardness of heart, he turneth to him that was aforetime politically-incorrect and saith unto him, "Say ye that these Fogeys and even these that are Old Farts are bastards?"

And he saith, "Nay Facilitator, for that had been my custom in the days of my political-incorrectness. But now I say they are no more bastards but socially-excluded persons which requireth inclusion, compassion and caring."

And BOSSY saith unto him, "Thou hast well said. Sayest thou also that the Fogeys and the Old Farts have need of counselling?"

And he answereth, "Yea, Facilitator, for all have need of the counselling and of the re-education, awareness-training, consciousness-raising and therapy of every kind."

And the People marvelled and said among themselves, "Behold, now we know for a surety that he is verily the Latest Thing on Earth, for he maketh both the partially-sighted to see and the politically-incorrect to receive of their correctness."

CHAPTER XVI

And BOSSY draweth nigh unto Camden and, behold, Crispin the Five-Fruit-and-Vegetables Enforcer was there. But the press of the People was very great and Crispin crieth the cry of his enforcement in vain over the noise of the multitude.

And, behold, there was a man named Zacky, which was Chief among the Fogeys whom his kinsfolk and acquaintance called the Grand Old Buffer. And Zacky was desirous of seeing BOSSY, but could not for that he was vertically-challenged. He ran, therefore, and climbed up a lamp-post to see him, for he was to pass that way.

And Zacky was exceeding rich for that he doth have the monopoly in the cigarette manufacture, so he was known among men as Zacky-Tabaccy. And when BOSSY was come unto that place he looked up and saw him and saith, "Zacky, make haste and come down, for I must dine with thee this day!"

Therefore Zacky did grin and shimmy down the lamp-post like unto smartish, like.

And they came unto Crispin and gave him two pence and he rendered unto them ten pieces of fresh fruit and singeth to them a couple of verses of the jingle which wast commanded of the Healthy Eating Commissar.

But the People which was exceeding health-conscious and bum-clenchingly Politically-Correct, when they saw it they murmured and said, "This man eateth with Zacky-Tabaccy which is an outcast of the People for that he maketh the cancer sticks."

And Zacky, knowing what was in their hearts, saith unto BOSSY, "For thy sake I repent of my cigarette manufacture and hereby sell all my tobacco shares and donate the money to the Lesbian and Gay Christian Movement, for the pufta knocking shop which knocketh there in the very crypt and for the after-civil-partnerships piss-up."

When he heard these words, BOSSY saith, "This day shalt thou have four score Brownie points."

And all the People cried out, "Brill! Nicotine patches all round!"

Then cometh he unto the City and taketh his seat among the bankers. And lo, there were they which are called "Europhiles" there. And the People watched him to see what he would do.

And the Europhiles also watched him and sent forth physicians of that which is called "spin" from the household of the Bureaucrat that they might entangle him in his talk. And they say unto him, "Facilitator, we know that thou art a lover of the Latest Thing and art Politically-Correct in all things; tell us therefore, is it lawful to argue for the EU budget rebate or no?"

And this they said, tempting him, for they knew that the place was absolutely teeming with Fogeys and stinketh of the Old Farts Party, which are them that hate the EU.

But he, perceiving their craftiness, saith, "Why tempt ye me? Shew me a Euro."

And they shew it.

And he saith, "Whose image and superscription hath it?"

And one crieth, "They're all different! But this one hath something that looketh like a frigging gorilla on it!"

And he saith, "Render unto the EU, therefore, what is the EU's and unto the frigging gorilla that which is of the frigging gorilla."

And the physicians of that which is called "spin" departed, for they could not answer him a word to this saying. And the rumour of him spread abroad so that the Old Farts said, rejoicing, "Seest thou how he screwed the Europhiles!"

And some said, "Verily he hath not screwed the Europhiles." But others, "He screweth the Europhiles in the power of the Europhiles." And their witness agreed not together.

And, behold, they departed that region and came unto Hampstead Heath and dwelt among the puftas and brown-hatters there which cease not their groping and casual assignations in the daytime nor in the night-season also.

And he saith, "I say unto you that a man shall leave his wife and shall cleave unto his brother, and there shall be the great multitude of alternative lifestyles and sexual preferences; for this is the doing of the Latest Thing."

But Andy saith unto him, "Facilitator, be there they which join not themselves unto the company of the puftas and brown-hatters, nor to them which are called 'Lipstick Lesbians' or of the Dungarees Party?"

And he answereth and saith, "Yea, Andy, thou hast well spoken. There yet be those which *know* one another in the biblical sense. And these shall screw around, for this also is of that which is lifestyle."

But he saith, "Ah, Facilitator, but what shall a woman do if, after that she hath screwed around greatly according to thy word, she discovereth she be with child?"

And he saith, "As it is written, she shall go to the abortionist and verily he shall rip that which is within her untimely from her womb."

But Andy saith, "How shall these things be? For this is a hard saying, Facilitator. I know that thou art the Moderniser General and that it be a liberated thing for men and women to screw around; but it happeneth that there are so many which be with child, even a great multitude so that no man can number them. Is it lawful for them all, every woman, to get herself to the abortionist and for that which is within her to be ripped untimely from her womb? How can this be?"

And he saith, "It happeneth in the aforetime, when the days were evil, that after a woman had screwed around – as it is written in their language, 'and had her fun' – behold, she was compelled to deliver that which was within her; and, behold, her lifestyle wast buggered up no end.

"But in the days of our Progress, when the Modernisation is come and the miracles of modern science are available to all without discrimination and free on the NHS – then this that is called 'untimely ripped', what is it but the modern form of that which was aforetime called 'contraception'?"

Andy saith, "But, behold, Facilitator, they have already the contraceptive, that which is called 'the Pill'. For a surety, it doth not weigh heavily on a woman to take unto herself the Pill before she goeth forth on the razzle?"

But he was wroth and his countenance was darkened and he spake unto Andy, saying, "The modern women shall not be discomfited by that they should remember to take the Pill. Behold, ofttimes it be not expedient for them to remember it. And they shall in no wise bear the burden of remembering it; for that were to interfere with their lifestyle."

"But the children, Facilitator, they that are untimely ripped – what sayest thou concerning them?"

And he saith, "Suffer the little children."

And he took unto himself his groupies and began to speak of himself, how he would be delivered into the hands of the Old Farts and the Fogeys and that he would be mocked and satirised wickedly; but after three days he would make a comeback.

CHAPTER XVII

And when they drew nigh unto the Great City, and were come to the mount that is called Primrose Hill, BOSSY sent two of his groupies, saying unto them, "Go into those streets over against you and ye shall find a bicycle tied to a lamp-post there, and another bicycle (actually a slightly older model) with it. Loose them and bring them unto me. And if any man say aught unto you, ye shall say, 'The Facilitator hath need of them.'"

All this was done that it might be fulfilled which was spoken of the Facilitator by the Green Guru, saying, "Tell them all in the Great City, behold, thy Moderniser General cometh unto thee, Green and riding a bike; and with a slightly older model of a bike."

And the groupies went and did as BOSSY commanded them, and brought the new bike and the old bike (with the regulation

Day-Glo waterproofs and the crash helmets, according as it is written in section three (Attire) of the Regulations for Cyclists). And BOSSY sat thereon and did enter even into the Great City.

And a very great multitude threw their teddy bears in the way, and others cast floral tributes in his path and cried, saying, "Cheers to the Moderniser General! Cool is he that cometh in the name of the Latest Thing! Cheers all round, mate!"

And when he was come into the City, the whole place was, like, euphoric and freaked out, saying, "Who's this guy then? And what manner of guy is he?"

And the Chief Apparatchik, together with the BBC Link Man in his clown costume, cried out, saying, "This is BOSSY, the Guru from Southend, the Tsar for Political-Correctness and the Moderniser General."

And BOSSY entered into Broadcasting House and cast out all them that made elitist programmes and which did the "talking heads" documentaries which were in the old time. And he overthrew the lap-tops of them that brought forth the classical concerts and produced serious talks.

And he saith unto them, "It is written, Broadcasting House shall be an house of noisy soundtracks and whirling captions, but ye have made it a den of elitism!"

And the partially-sighted and they that complaineth of all manner of fashionable neuroses came unto him; and he did counsel them all and send them with the alternative medicines even back to their own homes.

And, behold, he spake even unto the children that were obese, and said, "Get ye off the chicken nuggets and take unto yourselves the cabbage and cucumber!"

And all the children with one voice said, "Yuk!"

And when the Fogeys and the Old Farts saw the modern and progressive things that he did, and the children – even also them that were obese – doing their ethnic dancing in honour of him so that all their parents cooed and simpered and made the noise that is, in their language, written "Aaah!", they were sore displeased.

And all the unreconstructed reactionaries and conservatives said, "See ye not these things and hear ye not what things they cry out? It's not decent. Even the fatsos are doing it."

But he answered and said, "Yea, have ye never heard how it was written 'Out of the mouths of babes and suckling fatsos shall proceed hysterical ecstasies?'"

And he left them and went out of the City unto Tower Hamlets and lodged there, for he saith, "The days are come when all shall be modernised, irrespective of race, creed, colour, gender, sexual orientation or disability."

And they marvelled, and said, "How shall these things be, seeing that there be many which like not the modernisation?"

And he saith, "Behold, the Bureaucrat and the physicians of that which is called 'spin' shall compel them to be modernised. For with the Latest Thing all things are possible."

And in the morning, when he came again into the City, he was anhungered and seeth that the emporium which provideth the figs and the lentils, the sesame seeds and the aloe vera was closed – for they that had the emporium, behold, they had pissed off to the Live 8 concert.

He therefore enquired of them, saying, "Why do they that sell the figs and the lentils, the sesame seeds and even the aloe vera piss off to the Live 8 concert?"

And they say unto him, "For their heart is set on rooting out utterly all hunger in Africa and making the whole world a nice place and everybody happy, irrespective of race, creed, sexual orientation or disability."

But he saith, "But I'm one of the hungry! The bastards should have started with me."

And he was wroth and saith unto all them that stood by, "Let this emporium be no more an emporium, neither let them sell the figs and the lentils, the sesame seeds and even the aloe vera."

And, behold, he closeth it down under section four, subsection three, paragraph seven of the Food and Hygiene (Premises) Act.

And they marvelled, saying, "Behold, who is like unto the Moderniser General? For lo, no one doeth such modernisation unless the Latest Thing be with him."

But he saith unto them, "Why marvel ye that I said unto thee that this emporium shall be no more an emporium, neither sell the figs and the lentils, the sesame seeds and even the aloe vera? If ye had the regulations for healthy eating, even so much as a grain of sesame seed, ye would say unto this pie shop, 'Be thou shut down!' – and, behold, it shutteth down straightway; and unto this donut stall, 'Be thou no longer a donut stall!' and likewise it shall turn into a juice bar.

"And all things whatsoever ye do with compliance, continuous assessment and accountability shall be done unto you."

And when he was come into Broadcasting House, the Fogeys and the Old Farts enquired of him, saying, "Tell us by what authorisation is thy facilitating facilitated, O Facilitator? And according to which sections of the Standard Practice art thou standardised?"

But BOSSY answered them, and said, "I will also ask of you one thing, which if you tell me, I shall in like manner tell you by what authorisation mine own authority be authorised.

"For consider, the aquatherapy of Jak the Aquatherapist, whence was it – from the Fogeys or the Latest Thing?"

And they reasoned within themselves, saying, "If we shall say 'From the Fogeys', then he will say unto us, 'Then why did ye not believe it?' And if we say 'Of the Latest Thing' then we are in fear of the wrath of all the People, for all hold Jak as Guru of the Latest Thing."

And they therefore answered BOSSY, and said, "We cannot tell."

Then he saith, "Neither tell I you by what authorisation my authority be authorised."

And he spake unto them in spins, saying, "Did ye never read the Treaties which be from Rome and Maastricht and even Amsterdam, how the nation shall be removed from your authority according to the Constitution by which it is constituted? Therefore, I say unto you that when the European Superstate doth come, then your kingdom shall be no more your kingdom and your authority no more your authority. For the former things are passed away, according as it is written in the Constitution."

And, behold, they could not answer him unto any of these things.

And when the Fogeys and the Old Farts had heard his spins, they perceived that he spake of them and their doings. But when they sought to lay hands on him, they feared the People because the People took him for the Guru of the Latest Thing.

And BOSSY again spake unto them in his spin, and said, "The EU Superstate is like unto a certain Commissioner (not Man-Del-Son) which made a civil partnership ceremony for his son, and sent forth his officials to call them that were issued with freebies to come to the civil partnership ceremony; and they would not come.

"And again he sent forth his servants, saying, 'The French lamb and rocket salad are prepared, the disco is booked and the lines of charlie are laid out in the loos. Come, for all is now ready.'

"But they made light of it, for they said within themselves, 'Verily we have a better offer.'

"And the remnant took his officials and mocked them concerning the rocket salad and the shameless promos for all things Frog; and they did debag them and paint their very arses with the blue paint.

"And when the Commissioner heard thereof, he went ballistic and commanded his officials, saying, 'Slap fucking ASBOs on the whole fucking lot!'

"And they slappeth the fucking ASBOs on them.

"Then saith the Commissioner, 'The civil partnership ceremony is now ready, but they that were bidden were a bunch of twats. Go forth into the sink estates unto all them that are vulnerable and socially-excluded and which lacketh the table manners and bring them in.'

"So those officials went forth as he had commanded them and brought in all the oiks and yobbos and, behold, the civil partnership ceremony was furnished with guests which had not the table manners and stuffed themselves like there was no tomorrow.

"And when the Commissioner came in to see the guests, he saith, 'Bloody hell – where'd you find this sodding lot? I've gotta find some way of getting this swinish multitude off the premises. I am purposed what I shall do.'

"And he seeth a man there which was an illegal immigrant and saith unto him, 'How camest thou in here without a work permit?'

"But he was gobsmacked and saith, 'I wist not that I must needs furnish myself with the aforesaid work permit. I thought this was a piss-up.'

"And the Commissioner saith, 'Tag the bastard and chuck him out! For, behold, it is written in the European Constitution that care must be provided for the disadvantaged, the vulnerable, the underprivileged and the socially-excluded – but not in the palaces of the Commissioners, neither within many kilometres of their palaces.'"

CHAPTER XVIII

Then spake BOSSY unto the multitude and unto his groupies, saying, "The Fogeys and Old Farts do sit in the chief seats at the *Carlton Club* and in many other like clubs. And they clothe not themselves after the manner of the People – for they have neither the baseball cap nor the trainers. For they say, 'Verily we be not of the oiks, oikish; but put on the thick tweed suit or oft-times the striped trousers.'

"They eat not of the five portions of fruit every day, as the Five-Fruit-and-Vegetables Enforcer commandeth them. For they say this be food which is for the wild coneys (as it is said in their tongue, 'rabbit food') and take for themselves that which is called in their language the 'spotted dick' and 'bread and butter' pudding.

And verily they do smoke and go forth with the horses and hounds.

"All these abominations do they notwithstanding the continual importunings of propaganda from our State which is called 'Nanny'.

"Woe, therefore, unto the Fogeys and Old Farts which do say that there be no Narcissistic Personality Disorder, only that men are but selfish twats.

"Woe unto the Fogeys and Farts which say that men sin, when we do know, according to the gospel which was spoken unto us by the Guru Freud (which oft-times be written 'Fraud') that verily they are in the domination of that which is called 'Unconscious Motivation'.

"Woe unto the Old Farts and even unto the Fogeys which be exceeding judgmental and do say that there be sin and that it be very Original, and standeth in the following of Adam. For verily we believe that the People are nice and good and getting better all the time – as that which they that are called the *Beatles* do sing.

"And that, lo, it was the old time which verily doeth evil, but now that the Modernisation is come, we do know how smart we are and need not all that old morality crap. And that, lo, all it requireth is that every person be filled with self-esteem.

"For that it was said, 'Thou shalt not commit adultery', I say unto thee, behold, thou art that which is called 'liberated'. Go forth and screw whatsoever thou likest, be they man, woman or beast of the field – only see that thou wearest the condom.

"Woe unto the Farts and Fogeys which do say that the little children shall be governed according unto all that is given in the tradition wherein we do stand. For verily I say unto thee, take no thought of tradition, what thou shalt learn thereby in wisdom and understanding. And do thou give thyself and thy children unto that which is called 'creativity' and 'self-expression' and let it all hang out.

"For, behold, it was written aforetime that thou shalt keep all the sayings of the Lord in thine heart to love them and to obey; but I say unto thee: Believe what the sod thou likest, for, behold, it is written in the Great Modernisation and of them that teach it, 'Everyone hath the right to his or her own opinion – the no matter how sodding gormless.'

"Therefore, if the Farts and Fogeys say unto thee, 'Thou hast that which is true and good in the voice of the Scriptures and the worship of Him that is called The Lord', thou shalt say unto them, 'Be thou not so bloody elitist and chauvinistic. For verily we have also the Feng Shui and the Crystals and the Aromatherapy and all manner of that therapy which is called "Alternative"'.

"And if they shall say unto thee, 'Lo, here is the music which was sung unto us by our forefathers', do thou answer them and declare that thou wouldst rather the heavy metal and the grunge, for verily that which they do call 'headbanging', is it not equal unto that which is called Bach? And they that will not so say shall be condemned as elitist.

"And, behold, whosoever humbleth him or herself shall be judged lacking in self-esteem; but she or he that promoteth herself or himself shall become a celeb."

And BOSSY went out and departed from the BBC and his groupies came unto him for to show him the great buildings which were built in the City in the old time. And BOSSY saith unto them, "See ye all these old buildings? Verily I say unto you there shall not be left one stone standing upon another that shall not be thrown down and replaced by modern structures which be the machines for the People to live in.

"And, behold, there shall be no likeness among them, so that here a needle skyscraper and there a gherkin; here a concrete block like unto them that were built at Nuremberg in the days of their enslavement and at that which is called in their language 'Lubyanka'; there behold one with its innards on the outside wherein the walls shall be painted black."

But his groupies understood none of these things which he saith and, behold, their understanding was darkened and their eyes were closed concerning this saying. Then Bart saith unto him,

"O Facilitator, we know for a surety that thou hast wisdom passing the wisdom of any person – even Solomon which did build the temple. Tell us, therefore, surely the City will appear, as it is said among the infants and children, 'all higgledy-piggledy and that'.

"And, behold, they that dwell in the place which hath its innards on the outside, that is all black within, verily they shall grow pissed off so that they top themselves for very pissed-offness?"

But BOSSY rebuked him, and said, "Behold, I have told thee before: thou must become utterly infantilised or thou shalt not see the Great Modernisation."

And as he sat on Primrose Hill and did look down on the City, the groupies say unto him, "Tell us when shall these things be, and when shall the Great Modernisation appear. What signs shall there be?"

And he saith, "I say unto you, look not here for the Great Modernisation, or there. For the Modernisation is within you. And except ye be modernised in your heart, ye cannot enter into the New Project, neither into the Infantilisation which is amongst you already, nor the Great Modernisation by which all shall be modernised.

"But take heed that none deceive you. For many shall come from the East End and from the West End and shall say, 'I am the Great Moderniser' and shall deceive many.

"But there shall be signs over the air and in the www. When ye see that the People do put on their red noses, then know ye for a surety that *Red Nose Day* draweth nigh. And when ye do behold how they paint their faces and camp themselves up all along the street that is called Piccadilly, then ye know also that *Gay Pride Day* cometh upon you.

"So likewise when ye see the former things, how they pass away, then know that the Great Modernisation is upon you. For in the old time it was said, 'We have the Law of the Lord and by this shall all men be judged, whether they depart into everlasting life or into the flames which die not.'

"But I say unto you that when the Spirit of Modernisation is come, there shall be no reward and no punishment, for there shall be no law. There shall be neither what was called 'praise' or 'blame', but only Fame. And there shall be neither right nor wrong, but only that which is called 'Lifestyle'. For behold of anything, is it not as good as another thing?

"And in the aforetime, they said, 'Give unto us the scrolls and the songs which were written by them that were renowned for their greatness.'

"But in the days of your Modernisation, they shall no more read the old scrolls which were renowned for the good which they did bestow, nor shall your singers sing the old songs. For all these things shall be done away with and the People shall read glossy crap and their ears shall hear the music that doeth thine head in.

"In those days the children shall not be rebuked, neither learn they their letters.

"For I am the Way, the Truth and the Life. The Way, lo, it is any way that a person pleaseth, and it shall be said they have their right to go that way. And the Truth – behold, the Truth is that there be no Truth, but what everyone thinketh in his or her own thinking. And the Life, it shall be that wherein everyone doth worship them that are called 'Celebs' and wherein they shall proceed from one humourless abasement unto the next. And, behold, they shall all be pissed.

"But woe unto you, Old Farts and Fogeys, which do say that the Modernisation is a vain thing which gladdeneth not the heart of man. For this ye shall be called 'Elitist' and depart into everlasting gloom. And, behold, ye shall be marginalised.

"For the days shall come that there shall be no more 'elitism' but only that which is called 'accessibility'; neither 'classic' but what, if it be not 'pop' and 'rock' is 'crossover'. And if anyone shall say, 'Lo, this be a work of art, or that', then so shall it be."

And they asked him, "When shall these things be?"

And he saith, "Behold, there shall be earthquakes in divers

places, the sea and the waves roaring – for Global Warming shall be over all the Earth.

"And when Political-Correctness is preached in all the whole world, then shall the Great Modernisation come."

CHAPTER XIX

And, behold, he taketh aside his groupies, and saith, "The Narrative which I do spin is hid from them that are of the Fogeys and the Old Farts, that having eyes they see not and ears they hear not, lest they be converted and become Politically-Correct. But to you it is given to know the secrets of the spun Narrative, that, seeing, ye might become my apparatchiks and even be numbered among them that are my cronies.

"Ye that do ask for a sign, hear, therefore, the spun Narrative, and, hearing, understand. For then shall the Cloud Cuckoo Land be likened unto ten slappers which snorted their charlie and went unto the Feast of Glastonbury.

"And five of them were savvy and five were kooky.

"And they that were kooky were on the pull but took they no Pill with them. But the savvy, which were on the pull also, taketh them Pills plenteously.

"And lo, they begin all to screw themselves rotten until, at the last, they fell down, everyone pissed out of their heads and, like, totally shagged out.

"And it came to pass that, after many days, it ceased to be with the kooky after the manner of women and they were sore afraid, and they do cry one to another, 'Fuck me, Megan – or as it might be Amber or Jessica – I'm up the duff!'

"But they that had been savvy, behold, they were not up the duff, neither were they knocked up or bumped. And, behold, they do go forth a second time and even unto the third and fourth times unto the rock concert and the disco and do shag themselves exceeding rotten. And, behold, they are neither bumped nor up the duff.

"So it shall be with everyone that is totally modernised, for in those days they shall fear not to shag whomsoever cometh upon them in the daytime or in the night-season."

But Pete saith unto him, "'Ere, but look. Them that got up the duff, they could just have an abortion, couldn't they? Get rid of it?"

And BOSSY saith, "Oh yeah – I forgot! You got me there, Pete!"

Now it was the first Day of the *Festival of Di* and his groupies came unto him, and said, "Where wilt thou that we should book for our *Di Day* dinner?"

And he saith, "Do ye get on the phone and give unto Jason a bell. Enquire of him whether he can slot us in. Except it be not too late, for ye know I have a big day on the morrow."

But Phil saith, "Facilitator, let it not be the wholefood place, I beseech thee. For lo, the abundance of lentils is too great, and we fart, so that men do hold their noses and speak not with us. And it doeth naught for us with the totty likewise."

And Matty saith also, "Man shall not live by carrot juice alone, neither by the green things which be the coney food."

And Sim saith, "Say no more the wholefood place that is Jason's. Say rather that Chinky behind Smithfield."

But Jon crieth in a loud voice, "Let it not be that Chinky behind Smithfield – for verily aforetimes it giveth me Livingstone's Revenge, and that mightily."

And some said, "This place, Facilitator!" and others, "No, let it rather be that!" Save every one of them was of one mind that it might not be the frigging carrot juice again.

But he put them all to silence and saith, "For this cause have I chosen to drink the carrot juice with you and eat the lentils: for that the People fill the Great City on *Di Day* and, behold, they be very careful to watch the Facilitator to see what he will eat and what he will drink. And I must be an ensample to them, that they henceforth eat healthily."

When he heard these words, Pete was much discomfited and he saith, "Aw go on, just this once – the Smithfield Chinky!"

But he answered, "No. It is not for you to say 'Lo, let us go to the Chinky' or 'Behold, we haven't been for a curry for generations.' But that all might be fulfilled which is written of the Facilitator that in all things he doth live the healthy lifestyle."

And their hearts groaned within them. But Matty saith, "Nevertheless, Facilitator, let it be as thou dost desire."

And when the hour was come, they departed that place and came unto Jason's restaurant, even to the place of the wholefood and the carrot juice which is exceeding carroty and the lentils, behold, the which are full of farts.

Now when the *Festival of Di* was fully come he did sit down with his groupies. And as he did eat, he saith, "Verily I say unto you, one of you will shop me to the Old Farts."

But, hearing these things, Pete saith unto him, "Dunno about Old Farts, Facilitator: there's plenty of new farts in these 'ere lentils!"

But he rebuked him, saying, "Make no mockery, neither jesting which is not convenient."

But Pete saith unto him, "Aw c'mon it was only a joke!"

And BOSSY looked on Pete and, lo, he was exceeding sorrowful and saith unto him, "The days shall come, yea they are with us already, when there shall be no more jesting nor sayings that are not convenient. For lo, there shall be a new commandment which saith, 'Thou shalt not say anything which it happeneth might be offensive unto them that are obese or aesthetically-challenged or partially-sighted or hearing-impaired or differently-abled. Neither unto them that are of the wog religions or even unto them that do fart a lot.'"

When they heard these words, they all with one accord began to watch their backs.

And concerning him that should shop him unto the Old Farts, they all began to say, "Is it I, Facilitator?"

And he saith, "He that giveth me the second helping of farty lentils, it is he that shall shop me to the Old Farts!"

And he began to be much pleased and very jolly and his groupies were glad, even very glad, so that Andy saith, "Fuck me – I didn't know you could have such fun on carrot juice!"

And, as they were eating, BOSSY took the bowl of lentils and, making a New Age sign over it, ladleth it out unto the groupies and saith, "Whenever ye eat of the lentils, remember what exceeding good the fibre doeth for the prevention of the irritable bowel syndrome."

And he took the juicer and saith, "Remember thy carrot juice which is filled with carotene and that helpeth thee see in the dark.

"For I say unto you that I shall no more eat of the wholefood nor drink of the juices that come forth from the juicer until I eat and drink with you afresh when the Great Modernisation is come."

And when they had sung that old ballad by *Queen*, behold, they went unto the Mount that is called Primrose, and he saith, "All of ye shall be offended because of me this night. And lo, the Son of the Latest Thing shall be delivered into the hands of them that are politically-incorrect, and they shall mock him and satirise him. But after I make my comeback I will go with you unto Southend and unto the uttermost parts of Essex."

And they departed that place and went unto Kew Gardens. And when he had drawn apart from his groupies he began to be rather pissed off. And he remembereth his mantra which had been given unto him by the Guru. And he began to say within himself,

"Don't be pissed off, just go with the flow;
You're the Son of the Latest Thing, you know!"

And while he yet spake, behold, he that should betray him, even Jude the Fogey, drew nigh and kissed him.

And BOSSY saith, "Ooh, you are bold!"

And they came and laid hands on him and took him and led him away unto Poppy Pilates (which was called for his exceeding craftiness in the weird exercises) the Quiz Master and even unto the Broadcasting House wherein he must appear on the morrow.

And when the *Festival of Di* was fully come, they were all with one accord in Television Centre. And, behold, the damsels did come forth and dance their landmine dance. And the Presenter hollereth into the mike, "How beautiful are the feet that twinkle amidst the pretending landmines! Behold, Di – she would have died for it!"

When they heard these words, the great multitude of sentimentalists and them that were of the mawkish party did weep and cast forth their teddy bears. And divers of them tied ribbons all about the gaudy studio props. And, behold, he that was called Abomination of Desolation cometh forth and did sing *Candle in the Wind*.

And they call for Frugal Keen, which was the Co-ordinator Lachrymae, which did come forth and say, "Verily she was the Queen of Hearts! She was the People's Princess!" And of the tears that he did weep that day in the Television Centre were collected twelve firkins.

But the Fogeys murmured, "She did win prizes for throwing up."

But the People replied, "Behold, she was very caring."

And many cried out, "She was a very special person", and "Verily she was the People's Princess" and other such effusions. And the children danced the dance of the Princess's Frocks and sang the song of the Princess's Diamonds. And lo, they brought forth the very image of the landmine and did their obeisance before it.

And BOSSY stood before the Quiz Master which saith unto him, "Art thou the Son of the Latest Thing, the Moderniser General?"

And when he saw he was accused of the Fogeys and the Old Farts, he answered them nothing.

Then said Poppy Pilates unto him, "Answerest thou nothing? Behold, thou hast the second time this day despised the jackpot with the which our sponsors do sponsor our Quiz withal. Thou canst not hope to gain the prize if thou answerest nothing."

But he answered to him never a word, so that the Quiz Master marvelled, and said, "Phew, what a showstopper! Well, folks, I guess there's always a first time for everything!"

And being accustomed to, like, humourless abasements, the multitude did fall about, and say, "He hath of a surety more mirth than that which is called Ben Elton." And so spake they all.

Now, at the *Festival of Diana*, the Quiz Master was wont to bring on a "Special Candidate", whomsoever they would. And there was at that time in the studio one Darren Yobysczik which was famous in all the land for that he had won *Big Brother*. And Poppy Pilates saith unto them, "Whom will ye that I select to go forward for the jackpot? Press ye your 'select' buttons now."

And they do press them. And the whirling graphics revealed that they had selected Darren.

Then saith Pilates unto them, "And what shall we do, then, with this BOSSY which is called 'Facilitator' and 'Moderniser General'?"

And they all cry out, "Let him be satirised." (For the Fogeys and the Old Farts did psych up the People.)

But Poppy Pilates said, "Why? He's a regular kinda guy."

But they cried out the more, "Let him be satirised!"

And when Poppy Pilates saw that he could do nothing except that which the "select" button and the whirling graphics had shown to be verily the desire of the People, he did put forward Darren, which was called "Yob", for the jackpot, and BOSSY he delivered unto them to be satirised.

CHAPTER XX

Then the studio cool totty did take BOSSY and carry him into the midst of the studio. And, behold, there were lights of many colours and music abominable. And they mocked him there, saying, "We had thought that thou shouldst be the one which bringeth in the General Modernisation, but, behold, thou hast been knocked out in the preliminary round, as it is written, 'By the select button shall he be deselected.'"

And they put the yellow wellies on him and do bring forth the Booby Bonnet and lay it upon his head. And they do pour over him the paint of many colours. And the canned laughter mocked him also.

And all his groupies departed, like unto the sheep, sheepishly, and left him alone – except for the studio audience and fifteen million viewers nationwide.

And after that they had taken the piss out of him, they took from off his feet the yellow wellies and the Booby Bonnet from off his head and led him away to be satirised.

And when they were come unto a game show that is called *Gollygosh!* they satirised him there.

And they did set up the studio banner and the superscription of his accusation: THIS IS BOSSY THE MODERNISER GENERAL.

And, behold, the Old Farts and the Fogeys which stood where he was satirised said also, "He modernised others. Himself he cannot modernise!"

Then were two stand-up comedians of the Politically-Correct kind also satirised with him – the one on his right hand and the other on his left. And one also took the piss, saying, "Thou that would make the People Politically-Correct, give us a presentation on compliance now!"

But the other which was satirised with him said, "Let him be. For we are justly satirised for that we weren't very funny. But this guy, behold, he hath had a fantastic run."

And after three hours of this, the studio lights did fail and all the People went "Ooh!" And when the engineers couldn't get the sodding lights to come on again, behold, all the People pissed off home.

Then BOSSY, knowing that he'd had a great run and that even the best contestants get deselected eventually (for the People do weary of them all and look for all things to be made new) did laugh and cry out, "OK, Latest Thing – bring it on, then!"

And when he had thus said, he departed unto the green room. And, behold, the cool totty did give him the full body massage and the reflexology with that which is called "camomile tea".

And when they saw that he had dozed off, they left him lying there.

Then cometh Mad Magda, early, while *Breakfast TV* had not yet started, unto the studio. And she seeth two guys in white apparel cleaning the loo and they say unto her, "He's not here, lady – he's gone for an audition."

And Magda stood in the foyer twiddling her thumbs. And, behold, she was freaked out. And when she had turned back, she saw BOSSY and knew not that it was he.

And BOSSY saith unto her, "Baby, why art thou freaked out and, like, wasted?"

But she, supposing him to be the Commissionaire, saith, "They've taken our kid off for an audition and I know not which bloody studio he's gone to."

And BOSSY saith unto her, "Magda!"

And she saith unto him, "My Facilitator and my Moderniser General!" Which, being interpreted is, "The Latest Thing on Earth".

But he saith unto her, "Don't touch me. For, behold, after that they had given me the camomile tea, the cool totty cracked a few bottles and we got rather a lot down our necks. I've got this king-sized hangover and exceeding crapulence, so that, like, you wouldn't believe."

And, behold, she departed from that place and came unto his groupies, and saith, "He's gone for an audition!"

After those days, BOSSY appeareth at sundry times and in divers places unto his groupies, and saith, "I am he that shall be called 'The Comeback Kid'.

"And go ye into the Great City and unto the uttermost parts of the European Superstate, preaching and teaching them Compliance, Standard Practice, Social Inclusion and Equal Opportunities for all, regardless of age, gender or disability.

"And lo, Political-Correctness is with you always, even unto the end of the world."

– END –